THE SMALL BIZ GUIDE

Common Sense Tips and Expert Advice to

Help Improve Your Small Business

BY

JIM HARRIS

Published by Book Writing Pioneer
Cover design by Book Writing Pioneer
ISBN: Printed in the United States

Dedication

(To Marian, my partner in everything.)

Acknowledgment

To all of you who have been shoulder to shoulder with me over the years, thank you doesn't seem sufficient. Blane, Dan D., Patty, Terry, Jay, Randy R., Doug A., Jay C., Josh, Bruce, Lisa, Natalie, Mamadou, Jamie, Dion, Ashley, Randy S., Sandy, Sandi, Carl, Bobby, Ken, Olin, Adam, David, Gary N., Jose, Charlie, Claudia, Vernon, Jeani, James, Arthur, Shane, Joe, Evelyn, Dan P., Steve L., Mike T., Darwin, Mike P., Brian, Rick, Sue, Julie, Kevin and many I am sure I have missed, you all are the best.

I want to thank those who played a significant role in my life and career but sadly are no longer with us. Thank you to Neil, Pete, Don, Horace, Ebbie, Edna, Jay A., Buster, Riley, Jan E., Jack W., Steve H., Harry, Dow, Ray W., and Gary O. I was blessed to know you.

Contents

Section 1

Introduction

Small business owners are among our nation's heroes. They provide services, create jobs, support your communities, generate taxes, purchase goods and services that help other small businesses succeed, and so much more.

Many who advise businesses have their experiences totally from the academic world, not the real world where you live, where rolling up one's sleeves is a prerequisite on most days. I am reminded of the 1986 film "Back to School." In it, Rodney Dangerfield's character is a very successful businessman who returns to college as a student to spend more time with his son. One of his first classes was a business class.

The professor, Dr. Bombay, takes the class through an exercise of creating a fictional company. In the process, it's evident that Bombay's knowledge comes from an academic background, while Rodney's character brings up issues and challenges from the real business world. Rodney asks what their product is, and the professor replies, "It doesn't matter." Rodney responds, "Try telling that to the bank." After a bit of back and forth between the two, Bombay asks the class where they should build their factory. Dangerfield's character replies, "Fantasyland!" Sadly, this parallels many who try to offer insight to today's business owners.

Over one-half of the population of our country does not know what it is to be a small business owner. They have been employees, and while there's certainly nothing wrong with that at all, they have no awareness of what it means to be where the buck absolutely stops, to have your personal money on the line, often your life's savings and consequently, the well-being of you and your family at stake with almost every decision you make. You don't have a boss behind you to "run things by," you don't just get to walk away without a blemish if things don't work out, and you certainly don't sleep at night as those who enjoy those safety nets do. As famed entrepreneur Lori Greiner (Shark Tank, QVC) so famously said, "Entrepreneurs are willing to work 80 hours a week to avoid working 40 hours a week."

According to the Small Business Administration, there are over 33 million small businesses in the US, or about 99.9% of all businesses. 27 million have zero employees other than the owner. Others employ almost half of our country's workforce. Almost five and a half million of those have 1-19 employees, and around 650,000 have 20-499 employees. Over the last quarter century, small businesses have been responsible for the creation of over thirteen million new jobs.

Sadly, around 22% of new small businesses fail in their first year. Over half will be gone before their third anniversary. According to the US Chamber of Commerce, the four most common reasons for those failures are:

Poor marketing initiatives: How do you effectively and with financial prudence get the correct message about your business in front of the correct target audience?

Inadequate Management: In most small businesses, the "team" may consist primarily of the owner. Sharpening your personal skillset is critical to ensuring your long-term viability.

Financing hurdles: Cash flow is a challenge for any new business, but even more so for smaller ones. This problem extends to other areas, like employee turnover, which can be one of a company's highest hidden costs.

Unproductive business planning: Knowing your market, your competitors, and their strengths and weaknesses, proper staffing, your business's online image and impression, and a clear understanding of what your business does are vital for you and your team to know clearly and thoroughly.

In this book, we aim to give you tips that can help you expand your tool set to maximize your performance in these four key areas based on real-world experiences, expert advice in other areas, and observations from my own life and career.

In the first section of this book, I've shared my anecdotal experiences to frame a particular point. In the second section, there are no anecdotes, just solid practices that will improve your bottom line. In the third, I've reached out to some contacts in my network who are experts in their fields, and they have contributed tips that I believe you will find most useful. I hope you can pick up some ideas from my experiences to help your business.

THE SMALL BIZ GUIDE

Section 2
My Stories and Lessons to be Learned

THE SMALL BIZ GUIDE

Chapter 1

'Born' Salespeople or Just Motivated Salespeople?

It's very common to hear people say, "I'm just not a salesperson, or I am not comfortable with sales." It's almost like they think that some of us were born with a gene that they are missing. If that indeed was the case, I would have been the worst salesperson ever.

I grew up in a small Southern town, 45 minutes from Atlanta, but culturally, it may as well have been across the country. When I was 19, I got a job selling cars in Roswell, which at the time was one of, if not the most, affluent suburbs. In those days, salespeople wore jackets and ties. My "business wardrobe" consisted of two polyester leisure suits, burgundy and lime green, coordinating shirts and ties, and one pair of tan platform-soled lace-ups from the disco era. Imagine the worst fashion image you have ever seen, and you'll get a clue about my "look."

I was a fish out of water, selling Chrysler products (Chrysler was on newspapers' front pages almost daily, touted as likely going out of business. This was not an easy sale when a customer's first question would often be how they would get their car worked on if Chrysler shutters) to folks who lived in giant homes, drove the nicest of cars, sported elegant jewelry: you get the picture. I had no common denominators with our customers.

I had minimal sales training, guessing that even though they gave me a chance, the management wasn't willing to dedicate a lot of resources to this "long shot." They did, however, tell me exactly what to say at every stage, with every customer, which I did verbatim. I remember working with one customer and being told by my manager, "If I tell you to piss on a customer's leg, I wanna hear three things: footsteps, a zipper coming down, and piss hitting a pant leg." I did what I was told, and the skinny kid from a small rural town became a "natural salesperson." In my second month, I was the sales leader.

After they saw that I had potential, I got some fashion advice and upped my style game, and my career continued there. The lesson is simple: there are no "natural" salespeople. Of the salespeople I've recruited and trained over the years, some of the most successful, and I mean REALLY successful, came from backgrounds like pipefitters, janitors, butchers, body and fender repairmen, welders, a full spectrum of non-sales positions and careers. What did they have in common? It wasn't a natural ability. They listened, learned, followed directions, and had a hunger for success.

On the other side of the "natural" salesperson issue is the fact that we all are natural salespeople if sufficiently motivated. Let me give you a story.

I'm eight years old and heading into the Christmas season. I've had minibikes for a few years, but I want a motorcycle. I have my eye on a yellow Yamaha 60 motocross bike on the showroom floor at Wright Brothers' Yamaha-BMW.

My mother's first response is a flat "no." Being an eight-year-old, I know there's a point where I can't push on the issue anymore, but I didn't sense that I was there just yet.

From the conversation where I was turned down, I gathered that the primary reasons were safety, getting distracted from my schoolwork, my grades suffering, tearing up the yard, and riding it unsupervised since both of my parents worked.

I set about gathering information to overcome all of those objections. One Saturday morning, after riding to town with my folks, I walked to Wright Brothers and picked up literature that touted safety. I also bought magazines that had information about that particular model's safety features and ratings of the safest helmets. In the days before the Internet, research was slow and cumbersome, but I was motivated.

I knew I had a window of time to convince them to make all of the arrangements, so I picked my time and put my plan together.

When I sat down with my folks, I presented them with information showing that the motorcycle I wanted them to buy me was safer than my mini-bike. When I added the safest helmet choice, I could see them moving slightly in my direction.

Then, I promised not to ride when they weren't home and made a pact that if my grades slipped even the tiniest bit, it would be parked until I improved. I would pay for my gas and maintenance by mowing lawns, and before I rode it at all, I would clear an area that was currently wooded near the house so as not to damage the yard.

I never got a yes, but on Christmas morning, I had a brand-new Yamaha 60 under the tree (actually, in the front yard, but the helmet under the tree gave it away). Was I a born salesperson, or was I just motivated? Haven't you done similar in your younger years? If so, were you a born salesperson then but not now? Instead of a born salesperson, I think we should say I was a "motivated person."

Chapter 2

We All Pick Up Trash

Do as I say, not as I do, is likely the worst example you can set for your team members. You should be knowledgeable about every aspect of your business and understand each process. No task should be beneath you.

As I shared before, my background is in auto dealerships. As I rose through the ranks, my style and clothing choices reflected my level of success. I have always loved clothes, and my income let me enjoy my passion.

That being said, on a busy Saturday in the dealerships, you may have seen me dressed in my suit, nice dress shoes, cufflinks, necktie, etc., washing and vacuuming sold cars for delivery. Your question is likely: Why?

In a dealership, sales often happen in chunks. A backlog can happen quickly when you have two or three members on your detailing team and sell five or six cars simultaneously. With salespeople and managers busy making deals, I was likely the most disposable member of the team. It seemed logical to jump in and help.

Simply put, salespeople waiting with their customers for their new car to be ready and complete the delivery can't start working with another customer and hopefully create another sale. The sooner the car is ready, the sooner the salesperson can complete their orientation and delivery, and the sooner they are freed up to sell another car, hopefully. Waiting a long time for delivery doesn't usually result in satisfied customers, either. A backlog can give buyer's remorse time to set in, run into other plans the customer may have, or give another dealership they've visited a chance to call and upset your deal.

The message you send to your staff of you as a business owner who isn't afraid to get your hands dirty is a positive one. It shows that you don't feel any task is beneath you, and you are willing to do whatever is needed to help business get done. It also makes it tough for them to think any particular task is beneath them when they see you do it.

I did the same with "lot parties" or when the team went out and rearranged our display, and the same with plowing snow, too. The concept of a team means everyone. I'll admit that I drew the line at helping the techs with repairs. That would have been disastrous beyond description.

As the business owner, it's very likely that your team members have an assessment of your financial situation that often exceeds reality just because you're the owner. Getting on the front lines and doing whatever is needed helps put you back in the real world in their minds.

A company as large as Disney embraces a similar philosophy. Founder Walt Disney was often seen picking up trash around his park, sending a positive message to his team members that he wasn't above any task. They're known for following the philosophy, "Everyone picks up trash, from CEO to janitor." It is widely accepted that this extends beyond that specific task to everyone doing whatever is necessary to ensure that their guests experience happiness throughout their visits.

While we're on the subject, it's also best not to refer to your team members as "working for you." "Working with you" or "We work together" is a better way to avoid making your team members feel less than you.

Chapter 3

Building an Aspirational Brand

Are you an aspirational brand or operation, and should you be? If you follow the higher-end watch market, you likely know it's been years since a customer could walk into an authorized Rolex retailer and leave with a new watch the same day. There is a wait; for some models, it can run into years. Rolex could easily manufacture more watches, so why don't they do precisely that and meet the demand?

Even though the crazy pandemic seller's market in the auto industry is waning, Range Rovers and Mercedes G Wagons, Porsche, and several other luxury brands are still commanding a premium over list price. With demand this high, why not produce more vehicles and sell more?

It's the same logic that ultra-high-end luxury goods retailers have employed for years, sometimes decades. Having a product with high demand and low availability increases the allure of the product and makes having that product a status symbol. For example, it's impossible to walk into a Hermes store and leave with a Birkin bag. You must have a history of buying other Hermes products before being considered. The current estimate is about $10,000 on purchases of scarves, jewelry, etc., before the leather goods manager even considers you for a bag. Even then, you likely won't get a choice of model, size or color.

This is certainly not a workable model for most businesses. Still, if you occupy the high end where quality and prestige are higher considerations for your customers than price, there may be some tips you can pick up from these luxury brands. These lessons can translate into more mainstream segments.

In 2013, my wife and I, who both came from fitness backgrounds (her much more so than me), decided to start a personal training business. Having little equipment and not wanting to speculate with a huge financial investment on an unproven venture, we started in our garage and with less than $3000 in gear.

Our community's average personal trainer rate was around $40 for a one-hour session. Clients were usually in charge of the relationship, frequently canceling their sessions at the last minute without penalty, getting to pay as they went, and, in short, leaving the trainer in an often unfavorable position.

Having no track record of success, we knew we would have to start at the lower end of the scale. We trained our first clients for $30 per half-hour session. We worked hard with and for these initial clients, and they made great progress. We used their success to market our program.

As our demand grew, we made a bold decision to defy industry norms. We implemented a radical new process to benefit our business and the clients in attaining their desired results. With any other trainers in town, you could walk in off the street, swipe your card and start training immediately. Our process started with potential clients purchasing an assessment session, which cost them $199 and required them to complete extensive documentation and submit it in advance. This session was described to them as not only a snapshot of their current physical condition but also an eval of their history and mindsets. The burden was on them to sell us on their readiness for our program and to convince us to accept them as clients. We would turn down a client that we felt was not prepared to make a genuine commitment.

Our new rates were approximately seven times the going rate in the area and had to be paid in a package that ran well into the thousands. We also mandated that clients follow our food plans, which they had to pay for, and our workout instructions on their non-session days without exception.

Failure to do so would result in a warning and next, them getting fired as a client if they did not follow the system. We explained to them upfront that they had their chances to do it their way and had not achieved success and that our approach is all-or-nothing—either they fully commit, or they can't be a client.

Our firm cancelation policy was covered upfront with the clients. If they canceled within 24 hours before their session start time, there was no refund, and they lost a session, regardless of the reason. If they ran late, they lost time, ending their session at the pre-designated end time. In no aspect was the client in control of the relationship.

That all likely sounds harsh for someone who wasn't involved and is only observing. There is no doubt that these changes made our lives much easier and incomes substantially higher, but, ironically, by taking control out of the client's hands and requiring them to invest enough so that they take the process seriously and get their compliance on all aspects of the plan, our clients experienced tremendous successes and were the big winners in the equation.

We had clients whose medical teams had told them that they would soon be wheelchair-bound but, in just a few weeks, were running a hundred miles a month or more. Another client who had been forced to use a wheelchair when traveling because she wasn't stable or strong enough to walk through airports was now not even bringing her chair when she traveled. Weight loss numbers were mind-boggling, especially for those who had previously tried every plan under the sun without success. Clients got off of meds for hypertension, diabetes, and other syndromes that they had been on for years. They became stronger, lighter, and healthier, and their quality of life improved tremendously. Clients with Parkinson's regained strength and mobility as well as lost pounds and inches. Seventy-year-olds could work out as hard as people a half-century younger. Their medical teams were amazed, and many of those doctors also became our clients. Referrals from the medical community were our largest source of clients.

These client stories got a lot of media attention around the South and beyond, which attracted new clients, some of whom even flew to their sessions twice a week. Our results were even covered in the United States Congressional Record. In an industry that was crowded, functioning at low hourly rates, and even at that was struggling to get clients, we became, in short order, a mid-six-figure business and an aspirational boutique brand.

Now, contrast all of that with what would have likely been the outcome if we hadn't dared to choose a different path. This model absolutely is not a fit for every business or every segment. Still, if you are a premium-level provider and have the results and reviews to substantiate your leadership in your segment, some of these steps may be right for you. You must promote your success stories, share great reviews, and build your brand and image to be consistent with the value you provide. It isn't easy to be your own cheerleader, and I get that, but as my grandfather once told me, it ain't bragging if it's true.

Don't neglect one essential fact: If you want to be an aspirational seller or service provider, you have to deliver on quality and experience.

There is one additional lesson from that venture. Being that we were at the high end of the cost scale, from time to time, we would encounter folks who really needed our help but economically said that they couldn't afford the tab. In several of these cases, feeling sympathetic, we would cut the price to accommodate what they shared with us that they could afford.

If we had to rate the progress of all of our clients, those who we "cut deals" were at the low end of the results scale. We began looking at the "why," and when we analyzed the individual cases, we learned the lesson that I am sharing here, and we stopped cutting deals.

Surprisingly, we still encountered those who expressed an inability to pay full price, yet they always found a way. When the cost was a struggle to fit in, those people who had to find corners to cut to fit training into their budget weren't going to waste that investment, and they really buckled down, prioritized their fitness, worked hard, and followed the program well. The commitment to the plan was drastically better than those we had discounted, and the clients enjoyed exceptional results.

The lesson is this: people tend to value things based on what they pay, not always what it's worth. Discounting your product or service may not consistently achieve your desired result and may diminish the value of your product and brand. Think it through before you start slashing prices.

THE SMALL BIZ GUIDE

Chapter 4

Reviews

I like to point out my personal good experiences on social media and Google, to help companies that put in that extra effort. Of the twenty-two reviews I have posted on Yelp, fourteen are five stars. Of the ones that are negative, the common denominator is an apathetic attitude on the part of the staff or being ignored altogether. Likewise, the common thread in the positive reviews is service.

I used a new HVAC contractor for the first time a couple of months ago. The experience was excellent, and I gave them an excellent review. Two weeks later, I received an email stating that my review had been seen over 500 times. That's a lot of potential benefit from one good experience. Another email two months later let me know that two thousand people had seen my review.

Not every business experience will result in a positive review from the customer. The proper handling of a negative review, however, can create an opportunity for the business to not only redeem itself but also turn the situation into a positive for both sides of the equation, possibly retain a customer, and show goodwill and solid business practices to prospective customers.

In my younger years, supporting a business meant spending your money there and possibly recommending it to your friends. That was about it. Fairly often, I'll see a post on a page I follow about a business closing. Usually, it's something like, "I can't believe ABC is shutting down. We loved that place."

Being the curious type that I am, I've started looking at the reviews on the Yelp page and social media of the failing business to see if the person lamenting the loss has done anything to help that business. In almost every case, the answer is no. In today's social media-driven world, if you like a business, you need to help them with reviews and engaging on their social media pages, or you could see the place you like just go away. It can be make or break in our current environment. If you are the business, find a way that works for you to get those reviews.

While people tend to feel overrun with requests for reviews in today's crazy market, there are still some effective ways to ask for them. Consider a sign at your register, something along the lines of this:

If you feel we deserve a five-star review, please give us one on Yelp, Facebook, or Google. If you don't think we deserve five stars, please let us know why, and we'll work on it. Show us a screenshot of your review and get a free__________. (appetizer, drink, discount, etc.) You can also add a QR code to the sign to make it easy for the customer.

Another option is to use a device like a Zappy card, which we cover in the technology section.

Soon after we moved to South Carolina, my wife, youngest daughter, and I visited a highly recommended local restaurant. Our experience was a disaster from one end to the other. It was election night, so it was far from crowded. The experience was so bad we never even got to have a meal during our half-hour-plus visit. The hostess, who was in the middle of greeting us, just took a phone call and walked away. We weren't off to the best start, but sometimes things do improve, so we waited.

When we finally headed toward a table, we were the only party in the upstairs section, at an eight-top table, while many four-tops were available downstairs. The upstairs ceiling was very low. I'm six feet five inches tall, and I had to watch my head as I moved. Once seated, we were ignored entirely. When we finally saw a staff member and asked them to send someone over, we were ignored again. We finally gave up and left.

The experience was so bad that I posted a review with very specific details on Yelp. The restaurant management never responded or took advantage of an opportunity to salvage us as customers. We've never been back.

When we left the terrible experience restaurant, we began calling around and looking for a reservation elsewhere. We got into a restaurant that has been serving the area for quite a while. We had an excellent experience and posted a review detailing our evening. Not only did the restaurant manager respond to our review and thank us, but our server did as well. These two extremely different reactions led to two very different customer relationships. You can likely guess where we've returned multiple times.

Reviews for your business should be monitored daily. Positive reviews should receive a reply thanking the poster for the review and their business. Negative reviews should be addressed immediately and often present an opportunity to turn the customer posting the bad review around, plus show anyone reading the review that yours is a business that cares.

Don't be afraid to share facts if the review is based on incorrect information. The internet is filled with businesses defending themselves with facts and readers turning on the original poster (person posting it) for being unfair or inaccurate.

Your operation is not always going to be perfect, and every customer will never be satisfied. When you make a mistake resulting in an unpleasant experience for your customer, own it. To paraphrase the great Lewis Grizzard, "The public, more often than not, will forgive a mistake, but likely won't forgive trying to wiggle out of one." Many politicians can attest to that.

Chapter 5

Always Say Thank You and In Those Words

I recall an adage from my early days in business. I'm unsure to whom this should be attributed, but it rings very true. "If you think customers are a pain, try doing without them for a while." That makes sense, right?

Could the two most powerful words in business be thank you? An experience I had, offers insight into two valuable lessons for business owners. Never neglect to say thank you, and never ever come across as too good to speak to those who make your business possible, your customers.

If you pay attention to how most of your transactions end today, you'll likely hear, "There you go." "Have a good day" or something along those lines, but thank you seems to be a dying tradition. Showing appreciation for a customer's business is paramount to satisfaction. If your customer is, like me, a baby boomer, any substitute for thank you will likely fall short. Even worse, when you get nothing from someone who should know better.

This experience is a great example of the lack of showing gratitude to a customer and coming across like you think you're above speaking with a customer.

I have been on a motorcycle for most of my life. Starting around age 6, on a Rupp mini-bike, life on two wheels is an ingrained passion.

When my wife and I retired to South Carolina in 2020, I was without a motorcycle and had been for a bit. One afternoon, as we were driving down a main thoroughfare, I saw a gorgeous used Heritage on the front line at a local dealer. She gave a thumbs-up to stopping for a look, so in we went.

I decided (with approval from the home office) to buy it. My wife's family had known the dealership's owners for decades, so I was expecting an easy and pleasant transaction.

The process took a day or so because I had to get my South Carolina license to be able to get insurance. When that was completed, I went in to pay for my new toy and pick it up.

I was led into the business office to write my check and complete the paperwork. As part of the sale, they had agreed to replace the current seat with one better suited to my large frame. The new seat had to be ordered, so the fact that I was owed the seat needed to be documented on a "We Owe, which is a form that lays out anything due to the customer.

The business manager had to call the General Manager in to sign the form, as I guess he wasn't authorized to do so. The GM came into the office, asked the manager for the form, signed it, turned and left. He never spoke to me, acknowledged me, thanked me for my business, or anything else. I paid and left, but not with the best taste in my mouth about the dealer and especially the General Manager.

I went back in once after taking delivery to purchase a pair of glasses. My wife Marian and I started a conversation with the young lady who was helping us, and she shared that she was looking for another job because the GM talked to the staff in a very derogatory and unprofessional way. This confirmed what I suspected from my experience and was the end of my relationship with that dealership.

Since then, I have purchased four more Harleys and thousands of dollars in parts. None were from this dealer. I drive a half hour further in each direction to patronize a business where I feel appreciated. I have also referred many friends elsewhere for their motorcycle purchases.

There's also the consideration of what else I will likely spend in the future, not to mention the goodwill and business that could have resulted from my positive reviews, which I post frequently. As it turns out, the lack of a simple handshake and the two words, thank you, cost this dealer a customer, positive reviews, and a fair amount of future revenue. Multiply this times the other times this has likely happened, and it can add up to a tidy sum.

At the end of the day, a business owner or manager should never neglect to speak to a customer and thank them for their business. Even if it is because you are busy and preoccupied with another task or issue, it easily comes across as somewhat elitist and can sour a customer quickly.

I like to point out my good experiences on social media and Google to help companies that put in that extra effort. As I mentioned in the Reviews chapter, I used a new HVAC contractor for the first time a couple of months ago. The experience was excellent, and I gave them an excellent review. I received an email two months after posting that my review had already been seen over 1,000 times. That's a lot of potential benefit from one good experience.

This same principle also applies when dealing with your staff. According to Forbes, team members who are told "thank you" are half as likely to be looking for a new job. They are twice as likely to be engaged at work; they feel their work has meaning and purpose and are much happier at work.

In a 2014 study from the University of New South Wales, published in Emotion, researchers concluded that thanking a new acquaintance for their help makes them more likely to seek an ongoing social relationship with you. According to the study, expressing gratitude helped people develop new relationships, build on existing relationships, and maintain both. The person receiving the gratitude is more likely to share their contact info and the study also found that the person offering thanks was perceived as having a warmer personality.

Another survey by Sara Algoe of the University of North Carolina showed that uninvolved people who witnessed acts of gratitude also experienced a positive impression of those offering praise or appreciation. Algoe said, "Gratitude expression seems to be a unique kind of emotional experience that is really well-suited for relationship building."

Chick-fil-A received a lot of press recently for their policy of training their associates to respond to a thank you from a customer by saying, "My pleasure." That is certainly an idea worth snagging, along with training your team members to thank every customer or potential customer in every interaction. It's free, and the benefits are potentially huge.

Speaking to customers and offering thanks for their business is an opportunity to ensure that the customer feels appreciated, ask about their experience, and solicit what can often be helpful feedback.

Toward that end, I would be remiss if I did not thank you, the reader, for purchasing my book and investing your time in reading it. I hope you find some ideas here to help you succeed in your business.

Chapter 6

Lagniappe

Lagniappe is sourced in Spanish and Louisiana French and loosely translates to "A little something extra." These little somethings can be just that, but they are something in addition to what the customer paid for and expected and can go a long way toward turning the customer into a huge fan of your business.

A few weeks back, I found that a new sound mixing system I had ordered for recording my podcast wouldn't work with the cables I had. The company I purchased it from did not have the needed pieces in stock, so I located them from another company that showed to have them available.

Before I placed the order, I called their customer service to ensure the cables I was about to order would do what I needed, as the requirements were very unusual and specific. The rep I spoke with not only answered my questions but also emailed me the proper connection instructions while we were on the call. The service was better and more personal for the $20 cables than the much larger purchase of the soundboard.

I did not pay extra for expedited shipping, but my order arrived the next day, which was a very nice surprise. Included in the package was a small bag of sweet and sour candies, which I thought was a nice touch, and a personal thank you note.

Later that day, I got a call from the customer service rep who had helped me with the order. He was checking to see if everything connected properly and if I had any additional questions. Fortunately, all had gone well, and I was set and ready to record.

The amount of personal attention and service I received was far over what anyone would expect with a $20 purchase. I knew then that my future purchases in electronic needs would come from the business I purchased the cables from, not the one where I bought the control board.

Since that initial transaction, I purchased three other electronic items from the second store. The first business did absolutely nothing wrong, but the "something extra" from the second business, or lagniappe, got my attention, made me feel appreciated, and secured my future patronage.

In another situation, I had someone go above and beyond for me, and I wasn't even a customer yet. I went into Diamonds and Gold Direct to inquire about engraving an item. The piece I had wasn't made of a type of metal their equipment could engrave, but I bought another small item while I was there and had a pleasant experience.

The following week, I ordered an item online with engraving included. When it arrived, it was engraved on the wrong side. After contacting the seller without resolution, I took it to that local jeweler to see what they could do.

Since it was a PVD finish, they didn't have the proper equipment to engrave it. Nancy, who works there, asked me to let her see if she could find a solution. I left the piece with her. She tracked down a laser engraver, made arrangements to get the item to him, coordinated with him on what I wanted to be done, then picked it up when it was finished and met me to deliver it. It was perfectly done, and the level of service I received was what we may have experienced a few decades back but very rare today. I spent zero dollars with the local jeweler on this transaction but was treated like I spent a fortune.

I wrote a Five-Star review about Nancy and the company and the details of my experience on Facebook. It had dozens and dozens of comments and hundreds of likes and was seen by thousands.

Most business books and coaches agree that one of the most valuable assets that a business can have is a maven or someone who is so happy with your business that they not only recommend it when asked for a recommendation but also proactively promote your business through social media, referrals, and review sites. Experiences, like I described here, are lagniappe, or that little something extra. It's one of the best ways to create mavens. Take a look at your operation and find ways to provide that extra something and delight your customers.

Attention, appreciation, and going the extra mile go a long way in building customer relationships. A dealership I knew about sent a tin of chocolate chip cookies to each car buyer, which was nice, but I also felt the customer perceived it as an outside vendor, not so much a gesture of the dealership itself. A phone call from a manager would have cost much less and gotten more of a benefit.

Thank you notes have, for the most part, become a thing of the past. My wife Marian, however, taught our kids that sending thank you notes was not at all optional but mandatory. She does it herself as well. You would be surprised at the response from the recipients when they receive the personal notes.

Chapter 7

How Are Your Customers and Prospective Customers Being Handled?

How you think things happen in your business when you aren't around and how they really happen could be very different.

New car dealers around the country often belong to an association called the Twenty Group. It consists of twenty or so dealers who hold the same franchise, are of approximately the same size business, and are located geographically in a manner that doesn't make them competitors to the other members.

These groups would usually meet around three times each year. Financial analysis, idea sessions, and best practices dominated meetings. Sometimes, a vendor would be invited to make a presentation to the group.

In the 1980s and 1990s, the Internet was not yet around to provide information. While most customer interactions today may begin with an email, they often started with a phone call in those days. Given the importance of the phone in prospective sales, dealers had processes and policies regarding the proper way to handle calls and what information was acceptable, and most trained their staff members in properly using those techniques.

When a salesperson took a sales call, the only objective was to set an appointment for the customer to visit the dealership. In those days, cars were almost never sold remotely. Providing prices, interest rates, potential trade values, etc., was taboo, as providing them would only arm the customer to be a better negotiator on their call to the next dealer and likely keep them from visiting your dealership. Being able to set an appointment without providing the information the customer requested was a true art form.

Many salespeople, not seeing the potential value in a phone lead versus an in-person customer, would take the path of least resistance, provide the requested information, and likely miss the opportunity for a sale. If a customer visited our dealership armed with all of this information from the previous dealer, selling them a vehicle was a very easy and quick process.

Remember, times were very different then as far as being able to obtain information.

A company out of California specialized in working with their dealer accounts in phone training. One of their tools was something like a phone version of a mystery shopper. They would call the dealership's sales, service, and parts operations, posing as legitimate customers, and record the calls to be sent to the dealer for training purposes.

When this company made a pitch to a twenty group, it always went something like this. The presenter would ask if the dealers allowed their salespeople to discuss interest rates, pricing, trade values, exact availability, etc., on phone calls. Without exception, the dealers would strongly assert that they had well-trained people and did not do that. Their staff knew how to handle sales calls to be able to set appointments. Or so the dealers all thought.

After going around the room and hearing each dealer assure the presenter that their store did a great job and thus did not need their services, a phone would be brought to the center of the table and connected to a speaker. The presenter would then, one by one, call members' dealerships and ask for a salesperson posing as a customer. Group members would then listen to their salespeople doing exactly what they had just assured the presenter did not happen in their business. In short order, the vendor had each dealer signed up for their services. What the dealers thought was happening in their stores and how things really were could not have been further apart.

The point is not that providing information in today's environment is bad policy but that training and processes play a large part in how our customers and team members perceive our businesses. We need ways to check to ensure they are being followed. You need to be sure that your team handles customer interactions as you wish them to be handled. The phone may not be our customers' most frequent method of contact today, but the same philosophy applies to emails, texts, and messages through social media outlets.

Have you considered having your business mystery shopped? Seeing how email inquiries, phone calls, and in-person visits are handled can offer valuable insight into where your training efforts should be focused, whether your processes are being followed, and the impression your staff gives your customers and prospective customers. Hold times, the level of professionalism in call handling, showing appreciation for the customer's call, politeness, and many other aspects of customer handling can easily be discovered.

Before recording phone calls, you should check the laws in your state, as what is acceptable to record someone without their knowledge varies. One suggestion is to have all staff members sign an agreement and acknowledge that you reserve the right to mystery shop and record incoming calls for training. It is important that you positively use this information to try and develop your team's skills.

Using it in a punitive fashion will certainly get spread to all of the team members, and you could end up with no one wanting to take calls or respond to emails.

If yours is an operation that doesn't have a brick-and-mortar location for customers to visit, and/or your team makes calls to customer locations, it is still a simple matter to mystery shop your business. Have a business-savvy friend request your services without revealing the connection and ask them to evaluate their experience. Did the team member let the customer know an arrival time? Were they punctual? Did they look professional for the industry? Did they explain what was recommended and/or done on the visit? Did they answer the customer's questions thoroughly?

The point is that it's important to have processes for all modes of customer contact and to train your staff thoroughly. It is also imperative that you have a system in place to check and make sure that what you think is happening, really is.

As a trial, I decided to test out a random group of stores to see how they responded to email inquiries. I am a Big Green Egg fan, so I chose a question about the availability of a specific brand of charcoal I use for grilling.

National chains usually have their email contact forms set up corporately, not by individual stores, so contacting the local Ace Hardware, for example, wasn't a possibility. The same applied to big box retailers like Home Depot and Lowes.

The stores I contacted were across the country, in South Carolina, Georgia, Missouri, Kentucky, California, South Dakota, Montana, and Kansas. The inquiry was very short and simple, "Do you carry Fogo charcoal for Big Green Eggs?"

I sent out ten inquiries. In one case, the store had three locations. When I emailed the first one, I got a message that the domain name wasn't valid. I then tried a second address with the same response. Ironically, I did receive responses from both. The message I received may very well have deterred a real customer and caused them to reach out to another store, so that should be addressed.

Five of the stores had not yet answered after 72 hours. Of the five that did, three politely told me that they did not carry that brand, with no additional content to encourage me to become a customer. One of the responses was a perfect example: "No, sir, we do not." One of the stores with the error message let me know that they didn't carry that brand in their store but did in another location.

The best response, and the one closest to trying to encourage me to become a customer, was this one. "We don't stock FOGO, unfortunately, at any of our Hardware locations. However, our hardware locations can place a special order to get in a bag or so of the FOGO charcoal if you are interested in that as an option. If you stop by our ******, *****, *******, or ***** stores, our Hardware associates can assist you with getting some ordered for you! The item number that our team would need to find it quickly is #259966, but we can look around at other options that might be available to you in our catalog, too.

We do carry a number of different charcoals at our Hardware stores, though! We stock 2 of the Green Egg brand Charcoals (the original and their Eucalyptus blend bags) along with their flavored wood chips too. And at our *****, ******, and ***** locations, we carry a local brand of charcoal called Meat Head Charcoal. All of which are perfect for the Green Eggs!"

By comparison, this was, by all accounts, the most likely to get me into their store. Imagine if the associate had added a value incentive and call to action, something like this. "Our stores are very focused on the Big Green Egg and offering a wide variety of options and products for BGE users. I will give you my phone number, and if you let me know when you'll be coming into our store to check out our extensive selection of BGE products and the specific location, I'll let our team there know, and you'll receive a ten percent discount on your entire first purchase. Hope we see you soon."

Chapter 8

How Is It for Your Customer?

We live in a rural community, and our nearest grocery store is around ten miles away. When we first moved here, I was very satisfied with the store, even though the variety was less than we were accustomed to in a more metropolitan market. It was clean, the staff was always pleasant, and it worked for us.

We've all experienced the jam that happens in the checkout line when, for whatever reason, the cashier has to send someone to check or verify a price. Typically, those in line move to another cashier, and things resume moving.

With the changes resulting from the pandemic, most businesses are shorter-staffed than before. That came into play in a series of experiences I had in this particular store, and the lack of proper handling cost them a loyal customer.

As luck would have it, the price check scenario unfolded on FIVE consecutive visits. Unlike before, there were no alternative cashiers, and everything ground to a halt. The others and I, who were stuck in line, were left with no option but to wait until the associate returned from the far reaches of the store with the needed information. It was not a happy place, and the time wasted was significant.

My Mother always told me I should have more patience than anyone in the world because I had never used any of mine. She was definitely right, but the biggest part for me is when a business shows zero respect for their customers' time. In no way do I think this was malicious on the part of the store or management; I think no one had ever taken a proactive look at potential pain points in the customer experience and thought, "We should create a fix for that."

Now, imagine if the store had proactively created and implemented a process for this situation and trained their staff on it. The line would have continued moving, and customers may not have felt the displeasure they openly voiced when left with no option other than waiting.

Having established processes also leads to having happy and satisfied members on your team, because they feel comfortable in how they are expected to perform their duties. In a famous scene from the film Fast Times at Ridgemont High, Judge Reinhold's character Brad Hamilton loses his enviable job at All-American Burger because he loses his cool with a customer asking for his money back because he wasn't happy with his breakfast. "Brad" didn't know how to handle a refund, and in his frustration, used language he shouldn't have and got fired. Yes, it's a movie, but also a valuable lesson for business owners and managers.

Most of us would like for customer interactions to be handled by our staff the same way we would handle them. The path to making that happen has two parts. First, you need to have processes in place for every situation that may happen, then train your staff on those processes. If you think training existing staff consumes time and money, try constantly having to train new folks from zero.

Chapter 9

Is the customer always right, as you've often heard, or is that not 100% correct?

When I owned a Chrysler dealership in Atlanta, we had a couple of situations come up that taught me a valuable lesson.

In the first one, our service department had done an oil change on a Viper, which is a high-end performance car. The car wasn't purchased from us, and we had no history with the car, so this was the first visit.

Afterwards, the situation escalated to me after going through the ranks of our management, and the customer was still dissatisfied. The allegation was that, while changing the oil in the car, our technician had put his weight on the console and broken it. The Viper has a tight cockpit, so it is a bit challenging for a larger person to move around inside. The customer had spoken with the service writer, the shop foreman, and the service manager and still wasn't satisfied, so he eventually got to me.

All of our team members were empowered to do what they felt was right in any customer situation, so getting to me usually meant we believed the customer was in the wrong. After I spoke with the customer and got his side of the story, I went to our service team that had been involved for their version of events. The customer claimed that he had notified us of the issue shortly after picking up his car from service and that we had ignored his issue.

Everyone on our team who was involved had earned 100% of my trust over our time together, and when I talked with them, nothing matched the customer's version. If we had been responsible, we would have repaired his vehicle, no questions asked.

As a gesture of goodwill, after I concluded my research, I offered to give the customer the needed part at cost, around $1,500, and provide the labor for the repair for free. He declined.

The following week, I received a notice that he had filed a case against us in small claims court. I began to prepare for presenting our side.

When we got to court, he and his attorney were there with a box, presumably filled with his evidence. When our case's turn came up, the customer presented affidavits from several friends that backed up his story. However, none were there to testify to what they alleged, and the judge said, "This could easily be made up, and they all sound like they were written by the same person, so I won't consider those affidavits."

The customer's attorney represented the car as being an ultra-high value specialty vehicle and one that the slightest imperfection would cause a major loss in value. The judge asked for my response. Having researched the vehicle's history prior to our appearance, I was able to share with the judge that the customer had changed the car's color from the original factory red to yellow. A color change on this type of car damages the value worse than accident reports on CarFax. We also had still images from the video in our service drive when the car came in, and you could clearly see the aluminum rims were damaged from curbing. This was far from the perfect car the customer claimed.

Small claims court is much more informal than other courts, so the judge said to me that we had made our case and the customer had not, so he would leave the resolution up to me.

Until we appeared in court, I had never met the customer, but when I did; my gut told me he wasn't on the up and up, confirming what I had suspected. I had an idea that I thought would flush out whether or not he was being honest, once and for all.

I told the judge that, even though we had proven our case to his satisfaction, if the customer would simply provide his phone records showing that he had indeed called the dealership after he picked the car up, I would take care of 100% of the repair for him. His attorney bent over and whispered with him and then responded that it wasn't worth his client's time to do that.

The judge responded that the customer had hired an attorney, created affidavits and an evidence file, and taken several hours to appear in court. Still, one action that wouldn't take five minutes and cost nothing that would get him all he had asked for was beyond what he was willing to do. He said that the claim that he had called the dealership shortly after picking up his car was as incorrect as the rest of his claims. The judge wrapped up by saying that car dealers get a bad rap, but in this case, it was evident that the customer tried to set us up, looking for something for nothing, and we had done the right thing in how we handled the situation. The judge confirmed that the customer is not always right.

In that same time frame, the four-door Jeep Wrangler made its debut, and it was a white-hot seller. The brand-new design of the soft-top's operation was new and challenging for salespeople and previous Jeep owners alike.

We couldn't get enough of these vehicles. A competitor, a publicly traded company, was known for having salespeople who were notoriously undertrained, so they were delivering these vehicles to customers without properly demonstrating how the tops worked. Those uneducated customers began making their way into our service drive, looking for help.

At first, we tried to take the high road and help out, even though they hadn't purchased from us. Then, a new trend began emerging. Many of the folks had broken or damaged the ribs in their tops, trying to retract them improperly. They would then come to our service drive and ask for instructions, then try to allege we broke the top while demonstrating its proper operation.

We began to charge for the tutorial on vehicles purchased elsewhere and would not accept their vehicle until they had shown that the top's components had not been damaged. When you consider that this repair could run into the hundreds of dollars in parts cost alone, it was a necessary move. Sometimes, you have to make changes to protect your business.

Twenty or so years ago, electronics giant Best Buy hired consultant and Columbia professor Larry Selden to analyze their business and offer suggestions on ways to improve. One of Selden's main points contradicted most business's philosophies at the time and that was chasing sales volume. Selden recommended that the retailer focus on profitable relationships with their customers, and somewhat abandon those who only bought on sale items that were deeply discounted. Focusing on those more profitable relationships has allowed Best Buy to survive in a time when online selling competition is at an all-time high.

Another change was breaking a traditional taboo and discussing profits and margins with staff members. Bringing them into the narrative made it much easier for them to grasp the fact that profits were the way to ensure futures. You can read more in the book Selden co-authored with Geoff Colvin.

In it, they debunk the old adage that every customer is a valued customer. They state that in many locations, the top 20 percent of customers typically generate almost all the profit while the bottom 20 percent destroy value. Managers are missing tremendous opportunities if they are not aware of which of their customers are truly profitable and which are not.

The lesson here is that the customer is not always right. Toward that end, if someone has not purchased goods or services from you, then technically, they aren't customers yet. Perhaps a better way to phrase it is that the right customer is always right.

45

Chapter 10

Outside Vendors Are a Reflection of Your Business

Many businesses utilize vendors to assist in providing their goods or services to their customers. It is important to understand that, even though this may be an aspect of the relationship that is seemingly beyond your control, it can substantially impact the customer's opinion of your business. Oftentimes, those outside vendors can fall short of the mark, leaving the customer with a very bad taste in their mouth. I recently experienced such a situation.

Not long after we moved to our current residence, my wife and I were referred to a great doctor as our general physician. We were very positive about the relationship and referred many people to this practice. Last year, I got a call from their office saying my insurance company had denied a claim due to my policy not being valid at the time it was submitted. I called the doctor's office and left a message, but I never heard back from them. I assume this meant that everything was squared away, and the next time I had an appointment for a visit, they confirmed that that's exactly what happened. There was a mistake on the part of the company that they used to apply for claims, but it had been straightened out, the claim was paid, and all was good.

Early this year, I got a bill in the mail from my doctor for $1,300. I called and was told that, again, my insurance company had rejected it, showing my policy was not valid. I called my insurance company. They confirmed that my policy was indeed valid, and they also showed that no claims had been presented within the previous 120 days. I called my doctor's office back and left a message, but I have yet to hear back from them. I assumed that, once again, the situation had been rectified.

About a month later, my wife called for a regular appointment and was told they could not see her because we had an outstanding balance. I again called my insurance company and received the same confirmation that there had been no presentation of a claim and there had never been a time that our insurance had not been valid.

I called my doctor's office back and spoke with someone in the office who took a message to have the person who handles that type of thing call me back. Again, I never heard back. I assumed that since I had contacted the insurance agent again and had been assured everything was fine, the claim was paid, and all was good.

A couple of weeks later, I opened my mailbox, and to my surprise, there was another bill in there from my general practitioner for $1300. This time, I called my insurance provider and asked if we could jointly call the doctor's office to go over what they had told me multiple times.

It took three calls to finally reach someone, but when we did, the agent from my insurance company assured my doctor's office that no claim had been submitted for the visit that they claimed had gone unpaid. They also assured the doctor's office that our policy had never been invalid, not even for a moment. They showed in their records that every claim ever submitted against our policy over the six years we had been with them had been paid.

The staff member's response was not at all what I expected. The excuse I got was that the doctor's office used an outside billing service, and if there had been a mistake, it wasn't their fault but the fault of that service. At no time did the staff member apologize to me for having been accused of being a non-paying deadbeat, denying my wife her regular visit, or for all the time and trouble I had invested in straightening out their issue.

A few weeks later, my wife returned for a visit and asked to speak to the physician privately. When she shared the details of the situation and explained to the doctor that I would not be returning due to the absence of an apology, the doctor explained to my wife that it wasn't their problem. It was the fault of a service that they used, and no apology was offered.

Keep in mind that I was a patient of the doctor, not a customer of the billing agency. I had quite a few hours invested attempting to straighten up an issue that was not my fault. Multiple messages were not returned, and despite all of that, they were very clear that no apology was forthcoming.

A patient is also a customer, so if I deal with your business, who you choose to deal with on my behalf to deliver the product or service that I pay you for is not my concern. As a business owner or manager, it would be wise to pay attention to that vendor's performance because poor performance can cause you to lose a customer. From the customer's point of view, if I pay you, you deliver. Whatever you have to do behind the scenes to make that happen, it's not a direct relationship for me.

I am no longer a patient of the provider. This could have been avoided by paying attention when I brought the issue to their attention, researching it, and, at the very least, apologizing for disregarding my efforts to address it or wasting my time. I could have put it behind me and moved forward with a simple apology, but that was their choice, and they lost a patient as a result.

Many of you have shipping online orders as a component of your business. This is another area ripe for dissatisfaction and is sourced from outside vendors. Many people are like me; when they place an online order, even if it's something mundane, they get excited about their purchase being delivered. It's almost a high when, not long after placing an order, you get an email letting you know it has been shipped.

Your excitement cools when you see that, often for multiple days, the status shows something like "Label created. Waiting for pickup by carrier". Suddenly, it seems like your order has fallen into an abyss. Even if you, the business, do everything properly, your customers' excitement will waver if the delivery seems slow. I can assure you that I have NEVER encountered someone who experienced this and doesn't think of it as a negative.

This is another example of why you should evaluate every part of the customer process and ensure that it is structured to create and keep satisfied customers. It is also a great example of why you should perform a check on any vendor you utilize from time to time to ensure your customers are receiving a positive experience.

Chapter 11

Create a Win-Win So That Policy and Process Changes Will Be Successful

In every business, there will be situations in which you will have to, out of necessity, modify processes or practices. These changes may be unpopular with your team and/or your customers, so how you present the changes, help your team prepare for them, and train them in new ways will determine your success or failure.

Like every other for-profit business, the automobile industry's two biggest priorities are profitability and cash flow. It's easy to sit on the sidelines and think that every dealership in the country is rolling in money, but that isn't the case. Poorly run dealerships often lose money, lots of it, and struggle to keep the bills paid due to poor cash flow practices and processes.

In the early 1990s, I had been the General Manager of a dealership in a five dealership group and soon become a partner/owner. We had taken that individual store from a loser, profit-wise, to a big winner, upping the sales volume and margins drastically by building an amazing, talented team, and I received the opportunity to do the same with the group overall.

Because that first dealership had not been profitable for very long and we had recently increased our volume drastically, we were constantly struggling to get to the point where we had caught up from a cash flow standpoint. I looked at the sheet detailing our outstanding money one day and realized that we were owed over $500,000 from credit unions, just at that one store. The other four stores had similar situations. You might be shocked to learn how many businesses shutter their doors while showing to be profitable but run out of capital because they don't effectively manage their cash.

To put the importance of that $500,000 in perspective, the average used vehicle costs us around $12,000 at the time. If that half a million had been in our bank instead of outstanding, we could have added another forty-plus vehicles to our used inventory, drastically increasing our opportunity to add sales, gross profit, and new customers. If it had not been used to add inventory, that amount in a sweep account would add quite a nice chunk in earned interest over a year's time.

A little background to illustrate how that happens. In those days, credit unions had ridiculous loyalty from their members. When a member financed a vehicle purchase through their credit union, the credit union paid dealers by drafts. Those drafts did not become payment for the dealer until the new vehicle had been licensed in the buyer's name and the credit union's lien perfected on the title, protecting their security interest in the collateral. Those were called direct finance sources, as in the customer arranged it directly with the lender. When the customer was financed through a source that the dealer arranged, that was called indirect, and the dealer was paid immediately for the contract and received a fee from the lender for arranging the transaction.

For most dealers, new cars were floor-planned or financed by a bank. There was usually a two-day grace period for the dealer to pay off that encumbrance when the car was delivered, whether the dealer had been paid for the car or not. Failure to do so put the dealer in a position known as "out of trust," which could lead to suspension or loss of that credit line. Since licensing a car could take a week to ten days, cars financed with credit unions usually had to be paid off well before the dealer received the money for the transaction. At that time, the average new car was around $30,000, so it didn't take many deals to get into a cash pinch.

I did a deep dive into the process and decided that we as a group had to stop accepting outside finance sources like credit unions, as they were killing our cash flow and costing us the finance profit we would have made on those deals. One Thursday, I met with all of our General Managers and told them to roll out the new policy in their Friday morning sales meetings. There was pushback and concern about losing deals and customers, but no one could effectively argue against the cash flow aspect.

My lack of properly preparing our sales and management teams for the change led to that weekend being an unmitigated disaster. The following Monday, I pulled the new directive. I knew I'd be bringing it back, but it wasn't sustainable as it was.

I dug in and developed a word track and a worksheet for our salespeople to share with customers that illustrated the why behind the policy. Those with business backgrounds would understand, but I needed to be able to explain it to everyone.

I came up with an operational systemic solution as well. When our sales manager "penciled" a deal, which means starting the negotiation process with the customer through the salesperson, we began with two deal options instead of one. Option A was the price with the customer arranging their own financing, and option B with them financing through one of our sources.

When presented, almost without exception, the customer's response was, "Why is it more if I go through my credit union?" In the word track I created for our sales team, we responded that it wasn't more to go through your credit union but that we were willing to sell our car for less to get our money now versus charging the customer more and having to wait for it.

The example we showed was something like this.

$30,000 vehicle

$13,000 trade-in

$10,000 payoff on trade

$1,500 sale tax

When that car was delivered, we had taken in zero, as we couldn't even sell the trade until it was paid off and we got the clear title. So, within 48 hours of the customer's delivery, we had to pay off our bank for the new car, say $28,000.00. We had to send a check for the customer's trade-in pay-off, $10,000.00, and a check to the state for $1500.00 on taxes to get the new vehicle licensed. That puts us with $39,500.00 out and zero in. Multiply that times 20 deals and five dealerships and we're into the millions in monies out of pocket.

Once we successfully trained the word track, or script, to handle the objection, the issue seldom became a sticking point. I had to be firm that there would be zero exceptions because once you make exceptions to a policy, you no longer have that policy. Across all our dealerships, we likely lost no more than 4-5 deals a month total where the customer was adamant about financing through their own source. Our cash flow, however, made a dramatic improvement. With the $1000 per sale or so that we averaged in finance income of those deals that were previously going to credit unions, we added hundreds of thousands a year to the bottom line with almost zero downsides.

For any of you who look at the example and question the ethics, federal law at the time prohibited charging a higher price to those who financed with you than those who paid cash but had no restrictions at all about charging cash buyers more. Outside finance deals were considered cash as we didn't arrange them.

Lastly, it was only a short time until other area dealers began doing the same. The number of new cars financed by credit unions in short order fell to a level statewide of almost zero. Later, credit unions began paying dealers upfront and became indirect finance sources so dealers could arrange financing with a credit union through the dealer. The dealer got paid immediately and still made the income.

Another cash drain was in wholesale parts receivables. We sold parts to independent garages and body shops and had quite a large operation. Typically, we delivered the parts to them, and once a month, at a specified cutoff date, we ran a statement of what they owed and sent it to them. The customary policy was that they had thirty days to pay, and that timeframe often got stretched to sixty and beyond as they fought cash flow battles themselves.

We weren't the first to come up with this idea, but were the first to incorporate it in our part of the world. It was pretty radical in the days before the Internet when storing a card number was unheard of. We got card numbers from every wholesale customer in exchange for a slight increase in their discount amount. We ran a charge before we delivered the parts, and if there was any issue with their card, we addressed it before delivery, so we were always paid upfront. The good customers were happy because the extra discount helped their bottom lines, so it was a win-win.

Our cash flow improved drastically. We only lost a couple of accounts because of it, but they were habitual problems anyway. This type of change may not be applicable to your business, but the lesson is to think outside the box for ways to get your cash in-house and create a winning scenario for the customer in accepting your new policy or process.

The lesson is simple. You must evaluate your processes and policies regularly and sometimes will need to make changes. If the only answer you have as to why you're making them is because they benefit you, expect a failure. If you can present value in the change and train your team on it, you can make improvements and changes without major pushback.

Chapter 12

The Importance of Your Good Name

The Bible says, "A good name is to be chosen rather than great riches." Your character, reputation, and personal brand are inextricably intertwined. Who you are, who others think you are, and who you present yourself to be may have no lines dividing each aspect.

In the 1980s, I was managing a Chevrolet dealership and had to go to court to pursue collecting on a rather large bad check from a customer. The court session for my case immediately followed traffic court, which was still in session when I arrived in the courtroom.

The cases being heard were all about drivers not having proof of insurance or valid registrations. Case after case, if the cited driver provided proof of whichever missing document they were cited for, they were charged $5 for court costs, and their case was dismissed.

One of the last cases on the docket involved a young man who looked to be in his late teens or early twenties. Like the others, he had been cited for not having proof of insurance. As with the other cases, he provided proof of insurance, and the judge again instructed him to pay court costs of $5. As he had in all of the previous cases, he raised his gavel but stopped with it in midair.

He asked the young man his father's and his brother's names. The defendant answered. The judge said something to the effect of "Your family has been in and out of my court for years. You all never have insurance or registrations, don't license your vehicles, and basically refuse to follow the law. You, young man, seem to be following the lessons of your older family members. I sentence you to six months in county jail and assess a $300 fine." The gavel hammered out his words. Reputation ended up mattering to that young man, even though he didn't earn it personally.

The lesson is that we are all well served by acting in a way that creates and preserves our good name. This applies to your company as well.

Section 3
Solid Business Advice to Help You Succeed

Chapter 13

Understanding and Communicating Your 'Why': The Foundation of Your Business

One of the most critical elements guiding you in your business venture is your **"why."** Understanding why you started your business is essential, as it will shape or affect many of the decisions you make along the way.

Did you begin this journey because you had a passion for candle making, tennis, or scrapbooking? While these hobbies can make for delightful businesses, they may differ significantly from a venture that demands success to keep food on the table and a roof over your head.

Defining Your Purpose

Reflect on your motivations: Why did you start your business? Ideally, your answer should focus on fulfilling a need in the marketplace and developing a product that serves customers better than existing options.

Did you start with a business plan, or are you navigating this journey on the fly? If you did create a plan, are you still referring to it as a foundational guide, modifying it based on new insights as your business evolves? Or, like many, is it collecting dust in a drawer, forgotten since the grand opening?

As the old adage goes, **"You can't expect what you can't inspect."** This means that you need to quantify and monitor various aspects of your business to maximize profits and efficiencies. Imagine how the experience of a baseball game would change if no one kept score—it would be impossible to determine the winner.

Assessing Business Performance

Have you established a "report card" for your business? If not, this should be at the top of your to-do list. Key metrics to monitor consistently include:

- **Sales Performance**
- **Inventory Turnover**
- **Cash Flow (current and projected)**
- **Team Member Performance**
- **Net Profit and Trends**
- **Growth Metrics**

Understanding these elements can help you make informed decisions that align with your overarching business goals.

Evaluating Your Capital Investment

Did you invest sufficient capital at the outset, or did you open the doors with just enough to get started, leaving no cushion for payroll and other expenses? If you find yourself in the latter situation, don't feel disheartened—many small business owners share that experience. However, this realization should drive you to aim for better capitalization in the long run.

Articulating Your Vision

Before diving into any program to analyze and improve your business, I suggest you undertake one essential exercise. This step is crucial for your journey and will inform every choice you make moving forward.

Ask yourself this question: What four impressions do you want people to have about your business?

For example, a restaurant owner might answer: **1. Good food, 2. Excellent service, 3. Clean environment,** and **4. Professional and friendly staff.**

A hardware store owner could say: **1. Large selection, 2. Knowledgeable and personable staff, 3. Organized inventory,** and **4. Individual attention compared to big box stores.**

Integrating Your Vision into Decision-Making

The answers to this pivotal question should be incorporated into every decision you make from now on. Consider how your hiring practices, branding efforts, process implementations, potential expansions, and technology choices align with the impressions you want to create.

Can the people you recruit, the way you market your business, and the methods you adopt all contribute to achieving those positive perceptions? Keeping your "why" at the forefront will ensure that your business choices resonate with your goals and values.

Conclusion

Your "why" is the foundation of your business strategy. By consistently reflecting on it and allowing it to guide your decisions, you'll not only build a successful business but also create a brand that people respect and trust. Embrace this journey with clarity and purpose, and your business will thrive.

Chapter 14

The Most Important Investment as a Small Business Owner: You

When you started your small business, you faced numerous expenses to get things up and running—from logistical needs like inventory and point-of-sale systems to essential office equipment. However, all those investments pale in comparison to the most crucial one: **yourself**.

Leadership is the most valuable talent you can bring to the equation. If you watch any of those "Rescue" TV shows where a guru comes into a troubled bar or other operation, evaluates, implements a game plan, and sets about righting the ship, the assessment of the problems ALWAYS includes a lack of leadership. There's a lesson there as to the skill you should work on the most.

Abraham Lincoln wisely said, "Give me six hours to chop down a tree and I will spend the first four sharpening the axe." This applies directly to you and your business. Investing time in your education and preparation maximizes your ability to seize opportunities when they arise.

Wear Many Hats

Owning a small business requires a diverse skill set. Whether you're managing personnel, handling cash flow, marketing, branding, or overseeing operations, you need a solid foundation in various areas. Even if you hire specialists, having a basic understanding of their roles allows you to measure their competence and performance effectively.

Choose Your Educators Wisely

The first step is deciding where to get your education. Many "gurus" claim to offer easy paths to wealth and success, but be cautious. Often, they lack the skills they promote or are difficult to vet. Here's a perfect example.

In my previous career in the fitness industry, I encountered numerous advertisements from such individuals, especially one who showcased his lavish lifestyle—photos of exotic cars and stunning models in front of stately estates, suggesting these were the trappings of his success. It would add credibility as he attempted to sell very high-end consultation packages to fitness professionals. Despite our success, I was always looking at ways to help us continue to grow, and something about his approach intrigued me.

I followed him on social media but never signed up for any of his training, not being able to shake that feeling of "gut-instinct doubt" businesspeople often experience. I started seeing and hearing feedback from those who had paid for his services, revealing disappointing results, and the business advice they received was readily available from a simple Google search. Ultimately, a reputable consultant exposed his marketing tactics as a scam, revealing rented cars, homes, and companion imagery that totally misrepresented his success. Unfortunately, those who were less cynical lost their hard-earned cash forever.

The Value of Genuine Guidance

This experience underscores the importance of doing your homework before investing in a mentor or program. Seek educators with proven track records and genuine expertise.

Classic books by legendary authors like Dale Carnegie, Brian Tracy, Tony Robbins, Stephen Covey, and Napoleon Hill offer invaluable, time-tested wisdom and should be part of your business education. Don't overlook guides specific to your industry, as well.

Building Your Network

You don't need a celebrity mentor to succeed. Since moving to South Carolina four years ago, I've connected with many talented individuals in my network who offer invaluable insights. We regularly exchange ideas and solutions to various challenges. Local chambers, municipality business associations, and trade associations are great networking opportunities and could be fruitful spots for finding mentors.

One key figure in my circle is Carl Sharperson, a former Navy football player, Marine aviator, and an accomplished executive. He has authored two books on leadership: **"Sharp Leadership: Overcome Adversity to Lead with Authenticity"** and **"Sharp Leadership: Parenting Principles for Rearing Young People."** A cancer survivor, Carl embodies the mantra, "Winners never quit, and quitters never win."

Timeless Leadership Principles

Carl teaches fundamental principles that include honesty, taking care of your people, following through on commitments, consistency, and fairness. While you may think you practice these values, it's essential to reflect on how consistently you apply them every day.

Carl's insights serve as a valuable "tune-up" for me, especially when I'm focused on "sharpening my axe."

Listen

One of the most vital and needed traits that Carl and I both prioritize is listening; yes, it is a component of leadership. You'll be shocked at your staff's changes in attitude when they sense your receptiveness to their thoughts, ideas, and feedback. One of the most frequent reasons for failure in large corporations is the number of layers between those on the front lines and those in executive suites. An issue gets passed through multiple layers of bureaucracy, and each one covers its own rear end that by the time it gets to the decision-maker, the version of the original problem is so altered that it is unrecognizable and impossible to fix.

Conclusion

Investing in your growth and surrounding yourself with genuine mentors and good resources is the key to thriving as a small business owner. Remember, your most critical investment should always be in yourself.

Chapter 15

Find Guidance and Mentorship in Quality People

Mentorship can be one of the most valuable assets in both your business and personal life. This crucial topic deserves attention, as mentors can significantly impact your journey. Always seek them out and don't hesitate to ask for help; those who make the best mentors often value the opportunity to give back because they have benefited from mentorship themselves.

Lessons from Personal Mentors

I was fortunate to have two major mentors who shaped my business development:

1. Pete Cardiges:

I met Pete when I was around 21 years old. He taught me the mechanics of business and sales, imparting lessons that extend well beyond the auto industry. Pete was an exceptional closer with a remarkable ability to uncover the true objections of customers. He excelled at building value to help customers make positive buying decisions. Unlike many of my teammates, I eagerly learned from his techniques, which helped me become the top producer on a 30-person salesforce. His influence underscored how crucial it is to learn from those who are seasoned in their fields.

2. Neil Huffman:

A decade later, I began working with Neil Huffman, who provided profound insights about the importance of people in business. Neil was always a sounding board, offering perspectives I hadn't considered. He emphasized that every decision should consider its impact on the people involved, creating an environment where everyone felt valued. His commitment to giving back has made me a better person.

Learning from Unexpected Sources

Mentorship doesn't only come from those older or with more years of experience. Everyone we meet presents a learning opportunity. Some of my greatest business lessons came from people who, at a glance, might seem to be a very unlikely source of that wisdom.

Don Irvin was a unique individual. He had been a body repairman for years and wanted an opportunity to get into sales and then move up. When I first met him, and he began working on me to give him that opportunity, little in that first impression offered any insight into that being a smart move.

Don was nothing like the person you would be looking for when interviewing prospective salespeople. I don't mean to sound negative, but he was not polished in appearance, speech, or manner. He had one quality that is desirable for those in sales, however. He was relentless.

A call from Don became a daily occurrence. He wore me down to the point that I ran out of reasons why hiring him wasn't a good idea. Our dealership was located in an affluent section of the city, and I did not see his rough look and style as a good fit, but I resigned myself to the fact that if I didn't give him a chance, I'd be talking to him every day for the rest of my life.

Don came to work and went through our training program. He hit the sales floor, and an amazing thing happened. What Don lacked in polish, he more than made up for in determination, desire, and willingness to learn, and those qualities served him well. In short order, Don became a top salesperson.

When he wasn't with a customer, Don was quizzing me or one of his sales managers about techniques, closes, and whatever would help him be a better salesperson. Most other salespeople had the attitude that if they greeted a customer and did not see them as buyers in a short period of time, they felt that they were wasting their efforts and wanted to let the non-buyer go on their way. Don was the opposite.

If he greeted a customer early in the morning, it might be in the afternoon before you saw him again, but you could bet there would be a deal sometime that day. Don never hesitated to spend time building value with his customers, and they recognized that he was willing to cover all bases to help them make the right choice. We usually made higher profits on his customers than our averages, but his buyers loved him and referred their friends.

Over time, Don was promoted into management. I can't say that his level of polish improved, but by that time, it became evident that it didn't matter so much. Don would spend hours and hours working with the salespeople in his charge and developed many that were very successful. This passion for training them was an extension of his commitment to better himself.

To say he was hard-headed would be an understatement. When he came to me with an idea or something he wanted to try, if I didn't necessarily agree, telling him no was an all-day job. His passion and drive were always upfront and never abated.

He was never intimidated by anyone. I remember once that a college professor in economics was trying to buy a car, but the salesperson wasn't making any progress. Don went in to talk to the man, and I held my breath. These two people could not have been any more different, and Don, with little formal education in the matter, was talking about finance with a man formerly and extensively educated to do just that for a living.

As was typical with Don, he stayed with the man for an hour before I finally saw him exiting the office with signed paperwork, a credit application and a check in hand. Never count Don out.

Later, just before the customer took delivery of his new car, he stuck his head in my office and said, "I don't know where you got Don, but you ought to see if there are any more like him."

My lessons from Don were not so much about business mechanics but more about refusing to back down from your goals and never giving up. Success is often just one more push away. We can easily find a rationale for giving up, but Don taught me that believing in yourself can overcome that thought and lead you to success. He was an overcomer of all odds against him and giving him a shot was one of the best decisions I ever made or was talked into. I am a much better man for working with Don.

Reflecting on Insights and Values

A memorable highlight of my career was dining with **Mary Kay Ash**, founder of Mary Kay Cosmetics. She famously said, "Pretend that every single person you meet has a sign around his or her neck that says, 'Make Me Feel Important.'" This approach is key for building connections and enhancing both professional and personal relationships. My wife faithfully follows this advice daily, and it truly makes a difference.

Additionally, my experience with **S. Truett Cathy**, the founder of Chick-fil-A, offered more invaluable lessons. His emphasis on "putting people before profits" instills the importance of caring for employees and customers alike. Happy employees foster satisfied customers, which is the essence of a successful business.

One common denominator with these two great inspirations was their commitment to giving back. As **Muhammad Ali** said, "Service to others is the rent we pay for our room here on earth." Giving of yourself enriches your life, often leading to greater rewards.

Conclusion

Investing in your growth and surrounding yourself with quality mentors will lead to greater success and fulfillment as a small business owner. Each interaction is an opportunity to learn, and by embracing mentorship, you can navigate challenges and create a thriving business culture.

Chapter 16

The Quick and the Dead

In business, a common axiom refers to "the quick and the dead." Rooted in biblical text, this phrase emphasizes the importance of acting swiftly and decisively—or risk being left behind by competitors. One crucial addition to this adage is that no opportunity remains idle for long. If you don't seize it, rest assured, a competitor will.

Overcoming Paralysis by Analysis

One challenge I find myself frequently overcoming is **paralysis by analysis**. I tend to be overly pragmatic, often getting consumed by anticipating every possible outcome. If I don't keep this tendency in check and remind myself that there's rarely a perfect path forward, and I may end up doing nothing. This indecision can be fatal in business, which aligns perfectly with the "dead" reference in this saying.

It's essential to avoid falling into this trap.

Understanding the Dichotomy

When we think about "the quick and the dead" in a business context, we can divide ourselves into two groups:

1. **The Passive**: This group is slow to react, uninvolved, and resistant to adaptation. They miss opportunities as they pass by.

2. **The Proactive**: This is the group you want to be part of. They are engaged, anticipatory, and act with urgency. They assess

circumstances, make informed decisions, and implement strategies quickly.

As Teddy Roosevelt famously said, "In any moment of decision, the best thing you can do is the right thing; the next best thing is the wrong thing; the worst thing you can do is nothing." This reflects the need for decisiveness in business.

Learning from the Past

Success does not guarantee immunity from becoming part of the "dead" in this equation. Consider Sears, once so dominant that the Justice Department contemplated breaking it up due to monopoly concerns. Sears owned brands like Dean Witter and Allstate Insurance, and its headquarters was a landmark skyscraper. Fast forward, now the company operates just 11 stores in the U.S., down from a high of 3,500.

The same can be said for Circuit City, which had so much cash at one point that it launched CarMax. Toys "R" Us was an ubiquitous giant in retail, even showcased in numerous Hollywood films. The Sharper Image was once cutting-edge, with its catalog a staple on tech enthusiasts' desks, yet it too has faded from prominence. These brands failed to stay current with changing landscapes. Their decline serves as a poignant lesson: always keep your ear to the ground and your eye on the horizon for emerging trends, new segments, and the shifts introduced by competitors.

Avoiding Complacency

The phrase **"We've always done it this way"** can be one of your worst enemies. It's easy to remain in your comfort zone and resist evolving processes, marketing strategies, or inventory management.

However, your customers may feel that change is necessary, and failing to adapt may alienate them.

Conclusion

Decisiveness is vital for small business owners. By embracing the quick—actively responding to opportunities and challenges—you not only position yourself for success but also protect your business from becoming stagnant or, worse, irrelevant. Remember to balance thorough analysis with timely decision-making and to remain open to evolving with your market.

Chapter 17
Optics, Facility Policies, and Perception: The Customer Experience

In the world of small business, customer perceptions are everything. Often, the impression you leave on customers can significantly influence their desire to return or recommend your services to others. While it may not often seem like it, the world of fashion offers valuable insights into branding and image, which can greatly impact customer perception.

Think back to a time when you visited a business and left with a negative impression. You might not have been able to pinpoint the reason for that feeling, but it lingered nonetheless. There was something about the experience that affected your subconscious, leaving you wishing to continue your search elsewhere. Understanding these perceptions and how to control them is essential for your business success.

Learning from Fashion: The Power of Presentation

In 1975, John Molloy released a groundbreaking book titled **"Dress For Success,"** which became foundational for professionals seeking to improve their image. Molloy explored how styles and fashion choices influence the impressions others form about us. He referred to this concept as **"wardrobe engineering."**

In one of Molloy's revealing experiments, he had participants evaluate two identical models dressed in the same attire, with the sole difference being the color of their raincoats—one beige and the other black. The findings were striking: people believed the model in the beige coat belonged to the upper middle class, while the model in black was perceived as lower middle class. A staggering **87%** of participants viewed the beige coat wearer as more prestigious. These results illustrate how perceptions operate on subconscious levels, reinforcing the importance of appearance in branding.

Molloy also examined the impact of IBM's **"white shirt only"** dress code. In a similar study, participants viewed images of professionally dressed individuals. Those wearing white shirts were attributed with greater moral strength by **87%** of respondents. While the white shirt alone was not the sole reason, it provided IBM with a distinctive edge in customer trust and respect during its heyday.

Applying the Lesson to Your Business

What can we learn from these experiences? The need for attention to detail can significantly affect customer perceptions. Customers can form impressions about your business and its staff without always being aware of the reasons behind those feelings. By anticipating the factors that create customer impressions—ranging from storefront aesthetics to employee attire and behavior—you can cultivate a more favorable opinion of your operation.

Establishing Policies that Reflect Your Values

When you operate a customer-facing business, having clear policies in place is paramount. Consider how you manage families with children. Expectations for behavior may vary significantly between a family-friendly restaurant and an upscale dining establishment, for example.

Recently, a Georgia restaurant faced backlash after implementing a surcharge for parents who failed to manage their children's behavior. This situation illustrates the balancing act that businesses face: creating a welcoming environment while ensuring a pleasant experience for all patrons. Establishing policies in advance and training your staff on how to handle such scenarios can protect your business's reputation and customer satisfaction.

Managing the Customer Environment

Be mindful of the everyday distractions that may interfere with customer experience. Loud noises—like ringing phones, kitchen beeping in a restaurant, or nearby conversations—can detract from what should be an enjoyable experience. You and your staff may hear them every day and have become immune to the noise, but that doesn't mean your customers won't notice.

During my time in the auto business, I learned a pivotal lesson about perceptions. When customers see a busy counter but notice employees taking breaks nearby, it can create a perception of inefficiency. Regardless of whether the business is adequately staffed, this optics issue can lead to negative impressions. Regularly assessing your operational environment and addressing potential distractions can create a more inviting atmosphere for your customers. Little things like ensuring staff members take their breaks out of the line of sight of customers and that all eating takes place out of that line of sight can avoid a negative perception.

Protecting Your Customer Relationships

Implementing clear communication policies can safeguard your business relationships. For example, require that all customer interactions occur through company-provided devices. This practice maintains professionalism and protects your customer base's information from getting into the hands of your competitors who might seek to poach staff or hire them after they leave your employ.

You might also consider maintaining detailed records of customer interactions and preferences, ensuring that your team can deliver personalized service and reinforcing customer loyalty.

Developing a Strong Brand Identity

Your website and digital presence are often the first impressions new customers will have of your business. Take care to ensure your online representation mirrors the quality and professionalism you deliver in-person. Every online interaction—whether on your website, social media platforms, or review sites—should reflect a unified brand identity. Consistency in messaging, visuals, and tone fosters trust and recognition.

Demand for Transparency

In today's market, consumers value transparency and ethical business practices. Make it a point to showcase in a prominent place in your facility any credentials or accolades your business has received. Trust signals, such as certifications or membership in reputable organizations, can enhance your credibility and reassure customers about their choice to engage with you.

Identifying and Addressing Customer Pain Points

To clarify, a **pain point** in this context does not refer to physical discomfort experienced by your customers—at least, we hope not! Instead, a pain point is any aspect of customer interaction that can lead to dissatisfaction or a negative impression of your business.

Recognizing Common Pain Points

Some pain points are immediately apparent. For example, long hold times when customers call for support create frustration. However, many pain points occur in processes that may seem seamless from your perspective but leave customers feeling differently.

Understanding Your Audience

If you cater to an older clientele, complicated online order forms can be significant barriers, causing potential customers to abandon their shopping carts without completing a purchase. Accessibility and ease of use are paramount.

As a frequent online shopper, I often turn to PayPal for checkout on sites I don't frequently visit. PayPal auto-populates my information, saving me the hassle of creating profiles or entering my address manually. When I encounter a site that, despite using PayPal, still asks for my details, I assess whether the product is essential. If not, I'm likely to leave the site altogether.

These conveniences—and the ease of doing business—are important considerations both online and in physical stores.

Shipping Expectations

Another common pain point arises during the shipping process. Many businesses rely on logistics vendors to minimize shipping costs, which can significantly affect customer experience.

Imagine this scenario discussed in a previous chapter: You place an order, receive a confirmation email, and shortly afterward, you get notified that your item has shipped. Excitement builds as you wait for your purchase to arrive. But then, reality hits. For days, you see a status like "label generated, awaiting pickup by carrier." The item is no longer in the seller's hands; it's stuck in the logistics pipeline.

Waiting longer than deemed reasonable for an item can frustrate customers. While the shipping delay may be the vendor's fault, the dissatisfaction often reflects back on your business. It's imperative to communicate clearly with customers about shipping timelines and any potential delays.

Industry-Specific Pain Points: The Auto Industry Example

As a former car dealer, I have witnessed firsthand many pain points that customers frequently encounter. One of the most significant is the time it takes to purchase a vehicle and get on the road.

For instance, waiting to enter the finance office can become a particularly frustrating aspect of the buying process. Even in a busy dealership, long wait times can lead to customer dissatisfaction despite the dealership's best efforts to streamline procedures. Unfortunately, constantly evolving forms and compliance requirements often hinder progress.

Taking Action

Identifying and addressing these pain points is crucial for enhancing your customer experience. Here are some strategies to consider:

1. **Streamline Processes**: Regularly review your customer interaction points and seek ways to reduce friction. Aim for simplicity and efficiency in your online and physical processes.

2. **Enhance Communication**: Keep customers informed throughout their journey—especially regarding shipping and wait times. Transparency builds trust.

3. **Gather Feedback**: Actively solicit feedback from your customers about their experiences, specifically asking about what they found challenging, frustrating, or unclear.

4. **Invest in Training**: Equip your staff with training focused on customer service excellence, ensuring they can promptly handle inquiries and resolve issues.

5. **Implement Technology**: Utilize tools like customer relationship management (CRM) systems to track and analyze customer interactions, leading to more personalized and efficient service.

By understanding and addressing your customers' pain points, you can enhance their overall experience and foster long-term loyalty. Ultimately, when you make an effort to identify and remedy the challenges customers face, you not only improve their perception of your business but also contribute to its sustained success.

Create a Daily Checklist

Here are some suggestions for items you may want to consider for your checklist.

For physical locations:

✓ When you drive into your parking lot, is it neat and clean?

✓ Is there proper signage to direct the customer where to go? Of course, you know where your entrance is, but would a first-time visitor figure it out easily?

✓ Is the grass, landscaping, and general area trimmed and well-kept? Are there dead plants and/or weeds?

✓ Are the lines that indicate directions and parking spaces clear and neat?

✓ If you are in a center with multiple businesses, can a customer easily distinguish which is yours? Do the other businesses keep their facilities up in a way that does not reflect negatively on yours?

✓ Is the lighting in front of your business all working properly?

✓ Does your storefront look clean and inviting? Do you have any cracked glass, peeling paint, old, faded posters, dated signage, trash, cigarette butts, etc.?

✓ Are your hours posted clearly so that after hours visitors will know when to return? Have your website and phone number been posted as well?

✓ Does your look give off a positive vibe? As with the outside checklist, do you have signage directing the customer to the needed area? If you are a restaurant, for example, do you have clearly visible signage to let people know whether to seat themselves or wait to be seated?

✓ Do you have light bulbs out? Would replacing fluorescent lighting with LED, for example, create a warmer look?

✓ Is everything clean? Do your floors need vacuuming or sweeping/ mopping/ shampooing/ polishing?

✓ If you have a waiting/customer seating area, do you have current and relevant reading materials? If you have a TV, is it on a channel that isn't likely to offend or be perceived as negative by your customers? You may be a fan of Fox, ESPN, CNBC, MSNBC, or CNN, but what if your customers aren't?

✓ If you have an inventory display, is it neat and orderly? Does the arrangement make sense as far as ease of locating what a customer may want?

✓ Does your space look neat and decluttered? Do you have unnecessary items that are visible?

✓ Restrooms are one of the most overlooked areas of a business that can have a major impact on a customer's perception. Check them regularly to ensure they are clean and stocked with all necessary products.

✓ You not only have to consider the customer's experience but also those who may accompany them. If your business caters to a primarily female clientele, do you have a sitting area for males that may accompany them, or vice versa? Do you have current reading materials so they have something to do while the other shops and won't be urging your customers to leave?

✓ Check your website daily. Ensure all links are working correctly, images display as they should, and the contact form works. Enlisting a monitoring service is a good idea, so you'll be advised immediately if your site goes down. This will have a small cost but is highly advantageous to losing customers and potential revenue. It's estimated that as many as 78% of prospective customers check out a business online as the first step in the process.

✔ If you see any bad reviews, investigate and respond as quickly as possible. Sometimes, the right response to a negative review can have as positive an impact as a five-star review.

Conclusion: The Impact of Customer Perceptions and Experiences

Optics and customer perceptions play a pivotal role in shaping your brand. By proactively managing your business's appearance, implementing clear policies, and continuously assessing the customer experience, you can build a positive reputation that fosters customer loyalty and encourages repeat business. Ultimately, consciously understanding and catering to customer perceptions will enhance your business's standing and performance.

Proactively consider situations where you may have to take a position that could offend the person creating the issue but may save the experiences of a larger number of customers.

Look at your entire operation as a customer would and evaluate anything tha could create a negative experience, even a subconscious one.

Chapter 18

Finding, Training, and Keeping the Right Staff

Finding, Training, and Keeping the Right Staff

Finding and retaining quality team members can be one of the most challenging aspects of running a small business. Since the pandemic, hiring has become increasingly difficult, but with the right strategies, you can stand out in a crowded market. Remember, the best time to address your staffing needs is before they become critical, so taking proactive steps is essential.

Think Outside the Box

One key to successful hiring is to think creatively. Pre-pandemic strategies, such as simply posting job ads and interviewing a handful of candidates, may no longer suffice. Consider that you may be overlooking formidable team members simply because they don't fit your preconceived image of the ideal hire.

To illustrate this, let me share my experience in the auto industry. We found more success hiring individuals without previous auto sales experience. Sometimes, those coming from other dealerships brought along bad habits that could undermine your existing team dynamics.

Four of the best salespeople I ever hired came from diverse backgrounds—a janitor, butcher, pipe fitter, and a body repairmen— who delivered impressive results. They were not only leaders on our staff but were among the country's top producers. Their common traits? A strong desire to succeed, a willingness to learn, and an eagerness to absorb knowledge. If I had passed on them due to a lack of sales background, I would have made costly mistakes.

Conversely, I once hired someone who looked the part of a successful salesperson—dressed impeccably with all the trappings of success, wearing Gucci loafers, a Rolex, a crisply pressed shirt, and a beautiful silk necktie—he looked like the guy we could put in a brochure. Despite my patience, he struggled and ultimately did not meet expectations. I later found that his professional appearance was funded by his successful wife and that his lack of performance had been a pattern in his career. His polished exterior couldn't compensate for his inability to sell.

Proactive Recruitment Strategies

There are creative ways to find talent, even when you're not actively hiring. Here are some effective strategies:

- **Spotlight Your Team**: Highlight current employees on social media. This not only shows appreciation but also positions your company as a great place to work, drawing interest from potential recruits before you even post an opening.

- **Employee Referral Bonuses**: Encourage your staff to recruit for you. Offer incentives for every successful referral—a financial bonus if their recommended candidate stays for a predetermined period.

- **Participate in Job Fairs**: Attend job fairs, bringing a current employee to help present the benefits of working with your team. Prospective hires often value the insight and testimony of actual team members more than what you might say as the owner.

- **Utilize Online and Social Media Platforms**: Promote your openings on your social media channels and encourage current employees to share these posts. It emphasizes a positive team culture and attracts like-minded candidates.

- **Engage Colleges and Trade Schools**: Reach out to local colleges or trade schools to connect with students seeking experience in their fields. Many are eager to apply their classroom knowledge in real-world situations.

- **Explore Employment Services**: Consider utilizing state employment services or temp agencies, which can have a roster of qualified candidates, potentially offering you more options than traditional job boards.

A Recruitment Bonus Suggestion

Create bonuses for your staff members to recruit for you. Here's a hypothetical hiring bonus for your current staff. If a team member recruits a potential hire, and you bring them on board after your usual hiring process, if they are still on the team in thirty days, the team member who referred them gets a $200 bonus. If that referral is still on board in ninety days, the recruiting team member gets another $200, and then $200 again if the new hire is still on board at six months. The amounts are certainly negotiable, but in today's environment, a cost of $600 for a longer-term hire is a bargain.

A Retention Bonus Suggestion

I got this idea from one of my mentors, and it was a win for the company and the team members. Accrue a bonus for each member, based on some standard that benefits the company. For example, in our case, we accrued $10 for each car sold. You could do it for every clock hour, provided the employee showed up on time and worked a full day, or you could calculate it on a performance metric.

That money accrues with each pay period, and the team member gets a regular statement showing the balance. On a predetermined date (ours was December 15th), the employee receives ½ of their balance as a payout/bonus, and the other half carries forward into the next year. For example, if the employee had a balance of $1000, they would receive $500 as their bonus, and the other $500 would carry forward. The following year, if that person earned $1000 again, their balance would be $1500, their payout $750, and the balance carried forward $750. For a person who stays with the team for an extended period, it can become a nice incentive; plus, it helps keep them immune from looking elsewhere, and they have a valid reason to stay with you.

The stipulations are that the employee has to be employed and in good standing to receive the bonus at the time of distribution. If they leave before a predetermined term, possibly ten years, they forfeit any unpaid portions. Remember, this is your money and is a bonus over their regular pay, so if they leave and lose it, they aren't losing any money they've earned.

As with any creative compensation program, it's always advisable to check with your legal and accounting professionals before implementing it.

The Importance of Training and Support

Once you've hired your team, investing in their training is crucial. Insufficient training is often a leading reason why employees leave. Acknowledge the ongoing need for training that goes beyond initial onboarding.

Training should include:

Product Knowledge: Ensure your staff is well-versed in your products and services. Consider sessions where they present products to you as they would prospective customers. Use only positive and constructive criticism as feedback to help them improve.

Sales Techniques: Reinforce sales skills regularly, including best practices and customer interaction training.

Building Value: Salespeople often blitz a prospective customer with a barrage of facts and specifics. With the right type of customer, this could be the best path. However, with most customers in most segments, visiting your store or site is a learning experience.

Train and retrain the acronym FAB (feature, advantage, benefit). A customer's internal question is always, "What's in it for me?" and this addresses exactly that.

When sharing a feature of a product or service with a prospect, don't just share the feature but expand on the advantages that feature can provide the customer.

I'll give you an example from my early days in automotive sales. In the 1980s, front-wheel drive was becoming very prevalent in passenger cars. The Ford Escort, Chrysler's K-cars and quite a few smaller imports utilized the technology and were red-hot sellers. The public was just learning about front wheel drive. That configuration necessitates a transverse-mounted engine.

Prior to front-wheel drive becoming commonplace, cars had transmissions behind the engine and rear ends as part of the drivetrain. Here is an example of FAB for front wheel drive versus rear wheel drive.

Salesperson- "This vehicle features front wheel drive (feature), which also means a transverse mounted engine, with all of the drive train components right up front. This design puts weight over the drive axle (advantage), giving better traction (benefit), and it does away with the usual tunnel through the passenger compartment, giving you better legroom (benefit). Because the components are more compact, the car weighs less, yielding better fuel economy (advantage), and saving you money at the pump (benefit). Having this weight up front also offers more protection in the event of a frontal impact, keeping you safer (benefit)."

I think you can see how explaining the value and advantages of the feature creates a valuable impression in the customer's mind versus just throwing it out there. It also avoids the assumption that the customer is up to speed on all of these features.

Let the Customer Tell You How to Best Help Them

There is an old adage, a quote attributed to Epictetus, that "God gives us two ears and one mouth, so we should listen twice as much as we talk." This couldn't be truer than in a sales situation.

The stereotypical salesperson is a fast-talking, slick type who looks a bit smarmy around the edges. In the real world of sales, this individual is likely a flop, where the top performers know how to listen, absorb, and ask questions to glean answers to help match up the customer with the right product or service for their needs.

Credibility and sincerity are huge components of this piece of the equation. Looking professionally before even making the introduction is vital. If it's an e-commerce conversation, the look of your site and the nature of your team's response to the inquiry is what sets the tone.

Regular check-ins and constructive feedback sessions with your team and individual members can empower employees to grow and adjust as needed, enhancing their confidence and your overall business success.

Retaining Your Talent

As much as it is important to hire well, retaining your team is equally vital. Here are some strategies to enhance retention:

- **One-on-One Meetings**: Hold regular sit-downs with team members to discuss their thoughts, career aspirations, and any concerns. An open forum fosters trust and communication.

- **Create a Positive Work Environment**: A positive culture where employees feel respected, heard, and valued encourages loyalty and reduces turnover.

- **Recognize and Reward Efforts**: Acknowledge hard work and contributions, whether through verbal praise, bonuses, or opportunities for advancement.

- **Be Transparent about Company Goals**: Share your business objectives and involve your team in how they can contribute to those goals. This practice builds a sense of ownership and accountability.

Creative Scheduling

Making sure you have sufficient coverage at peak times can be quite challenging. Vacations can be an extreme example. For many businesses, the peak business times align with the most desired vacation slots, leaving you short-handed and likely losing revenue.

Summer is typically the most desired vacation time and can also be the peak revenue season for businesses that cater to warm weather activities. For those segments that offer high-ticket items, like cars and specialized business equipment, the last week of the year can be the best on the calendar but also one of the most popular vacation requests.

One solution is to offer a bonus so your team members can schedule their vacations during non-peak times. Let's say the summer months are your busiest times when kids are out of school. If you offer a 50% bonus on vacation pay, you likely won't change the plans for parents with school-aged children, but those team members without children at home may find that the additional funds are a good trade-off for scheduling their vacations during times where you can better handle being short-handed.

You could also consider a variation for specific days of the week and/or weeks of the month. Realizing that money for staff expenses is already the largest expense for most businesses, one should be prudent in how you choose to spend, but in the case of maximizing coverage to increase sales and revenue during peak times, it may be justified.

Conclusion

Finding, training, and retaining the right staff is crucial for the success of your small business. By thinking outside the box while recruiting, investing in ongoing training, and fostering a positive environment, you'll not only build a strong team but also encourage loyalty and performance. Remember, a motivated and well-trained team will not only support your business goals but also create a thriving workplace where everyone can succeed.

Chapter 19

Inventory Management: Turning Stock into Cash

In the film *Wall Street*, Charlie Sheen's character Bud Fox reminds Gordon Gekko (Michael Douglas) of his mantra: **"Don't get emotional about stock."** When it comes to small businesses, applying this adage to your inventory is crucial.

One of the most common mistakes business owners make is viewing inventory merely as products. In reality, your inventory represents cash that's just sitting on a shelf and not contributing to your bottom line.

The Importance of Fresh Inventory

In the auto industry, successful dealerships adhere to strict guidelines regarding used vehicles and parts inventories. Typically, they implement a hard-and-fast rule: a vehicle cannot age beyond a certain number of days, usually 30, sometimes 45 or 60 days. The reasoning is straightforward—those aren't just cars and trucks; they are money. Fresh inventory sells more quickly and often yields higher profit margins. As vehicles age, they tend to be overlooked by staff, and their market value decreases, turning them into financial liabilities.

Several factors can contribute to a vehicle not selling, such as seasonal demand (think four-wheel drive in July or convertibles in January), mismatched equipment or color preferences among buyers, or simply lack of awareness about the vehicle's availability.

Additionally, pricing may be out of step with the current market. A savvy dealership analyzes the number of times a car is shown to determine whether it's failing to attract interest or if customers are simply walking away.

Regardless of the reason, don't hold onto slow-moving inventory without a plan. Whether by taking it to auction, cutting the price, or finding another avenue to convert it into cash, the worst strategy is to let it linger in hopes that it will somehow sell itself.

Understanding Market Value

Remember, an item's value is dictated by the market, not by what you paid or what an appraiser claims it's worth. Before the recent rise in real estate prices, you might have heard homeowners bragging about purchasing properties for less than their appraised values. If a house is appraised at $400,000 but has been on the market for a year with the highest offer at $350,000, that's what it's worth. Similarly, your inventory—whether it's computers, lawn equipment, sporting goods, or shoes—is valued based on what someone is willing to pay. Unsold items are simply dead weight on your capital.

Using Technology to Your Advantage

Today, numerous Point of Sale (POS) systems can help track inventory levels and aging products efficiently. If an item hasn't sold in months and isn't seasonal, it's time to take action.

Consider these strategies:

- **Rearrange Display Locations**: Sometimes, changing the layout of your merchandise can rekindle interest.

- **Offer Discounts or Promotions**: Provide incentives to encourage sales, such as limited-time discounts or bundling with popular items.

- **Create Incentives for Your Team**: Encourage your staff to sell aged inventory by introducing bonuses for any sales made.

- **Leverage Online Presence**: Feature promotions prominently on your website and social media to reach more customers.

The key is to proactively manage your inventory instead of waiting for capital to deplete. Remember, cash flow issues are a leading cause of small business failures.

Conclusion

Effective inventory management is about transforming stock into cash and ensuring your business remains agile. By regularly assessing your inventory and making informed decisions, you can avoid the pitfalls of overstocking and keep your capital working for you.

Chapter 20

Understanding Expenses and Profitability for Small Business Owners

As a business owner, it's crucial to have a firm grasp of your costs and expenses. While achieving healthy margins in gross profit is essential, understanding your operating costs is vital to your long-term success.

Assessing Costs: What's Your True Expense?

What does it truly cost to sell your products or provide your services? To begin with, calculate the daily expenses of running your business. What's the financial tab for opening your doors each day, and how does your income stack up against that number?

A Lesson from the Auto Industry

In the auto industry, maintaining profitability can seem daunting. For example, the average markup on a $50,000 vehicle may be less than $2,000, while the cost to sell that car often exceeds $3,000. This situation means that even if a customer pays the list price (which might happen during a high-demand period like the pandemic), the dealership can still incur losses on each sale when factoring in operating expenses.

Consider the expenses incurred by both new and used vehicle departments—rent, utilities, advertising, payroll, commissions, and support staff, among others. By dividing the total operational expenses by the number of cars sold, you can evaluate the true cost of selling each vehicle. If the daily operating cost is higher than what you earn in gross profit, you risk significant financial challenges.

Calculating Your Daily Operating Costs

You may not be able to calculate a per-unit sales cost as those in the auto industry, but you can determine your daily operating costs. For instance, if your monthly expenses average $50,000 and you're open 25 days a month, your daily cost of doing business is **$2,000**.

If you sell ten products with a gross profit of **$150** each (say, you sold ten vacuum cleaners for **$750** each, having purchased them for **$600** each), your gross profit totals **$1,500**. In this scenario, if your daily operating cost is $2,000, you may appear to have a good sales day, but your business is actually running at a loss of **$500**. Lowering your profit margins only increases this break-even target.

Fixed Expenses Matter Too

Keep in mind that fixed expenses accrue daily, regardless of whether you are open or closed. Costs like rent, taxes, insurance, and inventory carrying costs continue to impact your finances, even on non-operational days.

Understanding True Labor Costs

When assessing expenses, consider the total cost of each employee. For example, if you pay a team member **$20** per hour, the actual cost to your business is significantly higher. Employer contributions for federal and state payroll taxes, benefits such as health insurance, and workers' compensation can raise your effective labor cost by **25-40%**. This means that if an employee's hourly rate is $20, the actual cost could be anywhere from **$25** to **$28** per hour once these additional expenses are factored in.

Guide Your Spending with Profitability Metrics

If your net profit is **10%** of sales, use this as a guide when considering additional expenses, like hiring staff or ramping up advertising. For instance, to break even on an additional $3,000 expense, you'll need to generate **$30,000** in sales just to break even on that cost.

Key Definitions for Small Business Owners

- **Gross Profit**: The profit generated from sales after deducting the cost of goods sold. It does not take into account overhead or operating expenses.

- **Net Profit**: The profit remaining after all operating expenses, taxes, and costs have been deducted. Net profit reflects the actual profit of the business.

- **Cost of Sales**: The total overhead and operating costs associated with doing business. This is essential for understanding the profitability of each product sold.

- **Net to Sales**: The percentage of gross sales retained as net operating profit, critical for understanding financial health.

Utilizing Tools for Monitoring Expenses

Using tools like Google Sheets or Excel to create a financial spreadsheet can help you track daily performance. It's advisable to establish a monthly cutoff period for financial statements or Profit & Loss (P&L) reports, as identifying problems early/on-time is key to addressing them effectively. If you work with a bank for financing, they will likely require these reports, so proactive management of your financials is crucial.

Conclusion

Running a profitable business hinges on a comprehensive understanding of your expenses. By keeping a close eye on your operating costs, assessing true labor expenses, and utilizing tools to monitor financial performance, you can make informed decisions that help your business thrive. Remember, clarity around your expenses is fundamental to building a sustainable and profitable entity.

Chapter 21

Effective Website Management for Small Business Success

When it comes to running a small business, your website functions as a vital virtual storefront, much like your social media pages. It's essential to present your business in the best possible light.

With **75-90%** of prospective customers checking a business's online presence before making contact, having a well-structured website can make a significant difference. While creating a website can seem daunting and potentially expensive, understanding what makes an effective site is crucial.

Clarify Your Objectives

Before building your site, determine its primary goals:

- **Will you be selling products online?**

- **Or will the website serve as an informational hub to guide customers to contact you?**

Analyze competitor websites to see what elements appeal to you and identify opportunities for improvement.

Choose the Right Hosting Plan

Select a reliable hosting provider to ensure your website is accessible 24/7 with minimal downtime. A slow-loading site can drive potential customers away—nearly **half** will leave if a page takes longer than **two seconds** to load. Consider using image compression tools or plugins to enhance loading times.

Also, just as we mentioned in the social media chapter, restricting countries that can access your site can cut down drastically on spam and bots. Be sure and check with your hosting provider if this option is available for you.

Use protocols like Secure Socket Layer to protect your content and the customer's private information.

Make Key Information Accessible

Ensure that all critical information is prominently displayed on your website, including:

- Business hours

- Location (if applicable)

- Contact details (phone numbers, email, chat options)

This transparency minimizes customer frustration and makes it easy for them to reach out.

Showcase Your Reputation

Your website is an excellent platform to display positive reviews. Use plugins or features that automatically showcase reviews from platforms like Facebook, Yelp, or Google, making them easily accessible to visitors.

Use High-Quality Visuals

High-resolution images of your products, services, or physical location can significantly enhance your site's appeal. Ensure that visuals are clear and accurately represent what you offer.

Keep Content Current

Regularly update your website to avoid displaying outdated information. Missing images, broken links, or outdated promotional content can create a poor impression. For example, if your menu or prices change (especially for restaurants), ensure everything is aligned with what you offer to avoid disappointing customers.

Prioritize User-Friendly Layout

Avoid cluttering your website with excessive information. Use simple layouts and clear navigation, keeping paragraphs concise and easy to read—aim for sentences under twenty-five words and paragraphs no longer than four sentences.

Implement SEO Best Practices

Utilize your web host's SEO evaluation tools to optimize content with relevant keywords to boost search engine visibility. Investing time in learning basic SEO concepts is time well spent. Try to keep your sentences down to twenty-five words or fewer and paragraphs to four sentences.

Remove Outdated Content Promptly

Once time-sensitive offers expire, ensure that this content is removed immediately to avoid frustrating customers looking for outdated promotions.

Enhance Search Functionality

Incorporate a search feature on your website to help visitors easily find the information or products they seek.

Display Credentials and Trust Signals

If you have memberships or credentials from reputable organizations, such as the Better Business Bureau (BBB) or

Trustpilot, display these prominently. They enhance your credibility and trustworthiness.

Gather Feedback

Invite others to review your site from a newcomer's perspective. Solicit feedback on your layout, content, and overall user experience—this helps ensure that the website meets customer needs rather than just your preferences. Use keywords to help search engines find your content.

Optimize for Mobile Devices

Ensure your website is mobile-friendly. Given that a significant portion of visitors will access your site via phones or tablets, most website builders offer preview options to ensure compatibility across devices.

Provide Relevant Links and Resources

Use hyperlinks to guide visitors to related content. For instance, an auto parts store might link to a tutorial on installing a specific part, enhancing the user experience and authority.

Utilize Google Analytics

Implement tools like Google Analytics to gain insights into visitor behavior—such as their geographic location, peak visit times, device usage, and most viewed pages. Use this data to improve content and enhance marketing strategies. Strive for an increasing number of visitors each week and aim for longer session durations and multiple page views on your site.

Ensure Smooth Online Transactions

If you have an online store, regularly check that your purchasing system operates smoothly. Ensure that customers can easily add items to their cart, understand shipping options, and choose from various payment methods.

Conclusion: The Importance of Presentation and Detail

Your website is often the first impression customers have of your business. Every interaction—whether it's an online chat, a social media post, or an email—should reflect your commitment to quality and professionalism.

Mistakes can impact your reputation significantly. For instance, L.L. Bean once faced substantial costs due to a typo in their ads. They published the wrong phone number. To salvage the promotion, they had to pay the owner of the number shown in their promo piece a large sum to get them to give up the number. Another example of a mistake beyond the pale is when the Vatican ordered over 6,000 medals in honor of Pope Francis but misspelled Jesus instead, using Lesus. Similarly, ensure all communications are clear and accurate to prevent misunderstandings.

By paying attention to details and regularly optimizing your online presence, your business will not only attract but also retain customers, ultimately leading your business to greater success.

Chapter 22

Leveraging Technology for Small Business Success

In today's competitive landscape, utilizing technology effectively can significantly enhance your business operations. While technology will never replace the importance of people skills, the right tools and resources can help you manage your team, add value for your customers, and improve your brand.

An Easy Path to More Customer Reviews

Customers today are inundated with requests for reviews. However, these reviews are crucial: most prospective customers read them before contacting a business. If you're like many consumers who frequently make purchases, you may find your inbox overwhelmed with review requests. Thankfully, new products are emerging to streamline this process and increase your likelihood of gathering valuable feedback.

Google Review Cards are one such tool. These cards contain your business information and an embedded link to your Google Business page. Just tap the card against a customer's phone, and they receive an immediate notification prompting them to leave a review. This method can be employed by both brick-and-mortar stores and online providers at checkout, significantly boosting the number of reviews you receive. A simple Google search for "Google review cards" will show you various options, typically costing well under $100. Zappy and Tap Tag are among the best-known brands.

Digital Business Cards

Another innovative resource is the **digital business card**. Like review cards, these cards embed your contact information and can be shared via a tap or QR code. You can also link to your website, social media, and email. Many of these digital cards enable the recipient to easily share their contact info with you with one click, facilitating quicker networking. Dot and Ovou are well-known providers in that space.

Tracking Employee Activities

Managing teams requires oversight, especially for those with employees in the field. Knowing your team members' location can be invaluable for scheduling appointments and ensuring timely service.

Vehicle GPS tracking has existed for years, but if you provide work phones, consider installing tracking software to receive real-time location updates. This can also help monitor employee performance and customer interactions. Remember to navigate privacy and legal considerations while being transparent with your team about the software's use. Make your team members aware that you are utilizing this product before you begin using it.

It's always a good practice to ensure your customer contacts are being handled as you desire. Many companies utilize **call recording** features that inform all parties involved for a less invasive approach. Hearing, "Calls may be recorded for quality and training purposes," is common. This helps ensure that everyone is aware of the potential for recording. When we recorded sales calls, our salespeople would sign an acknowledgment of this policy.

Effective Communication

In a world where communication is key, utilizing **text messaging** can significantly improve how you interact with customers. Text messages boast higher open rates compared to emails, making them a powerful tool for sharing promotions, updates, or valuable information. Services offering text/SMS communication start free for a limited number of contacts and can typically be scaled up for under $100 per month.

With advancements in technology, **answering services** have evolved as well. Services like Smith.ai, Posh, and RingCentral combine AI with human staffing to ensure around-the-clock availability, enhancing your ability to serve customers without breaking the bank.

Virtual Assistants

Consider employing **virtual assistants (VAs)** to handle routine tasks, freeing you up to focus on revenue-generating opportunities. Hiring a VA can be a small investment with significant returns. This concept is reflected in the adage: "Don't get so caught up working in your business that you don't have time to work ON your business." Platforms like Fiverr can help you find the right talent to fit your needs.

Utilizing QR Codes

Just a few years ago, many of us over 40 might not have known what a **QR code** was. Today, they're ubiquitous. These codes offer an effortless way for customers to access your website or social media pages using their phones' cameras. Integrate QR codes into sales emails, newsletters, signs at events, and anywhere else you wish to connect with potential customers. While many QR code generators are free, customizing them can enhance your brand's professional appearance.

Short or tiny URLs can shorten your social media posts by eliminating the need for a long link in your copy. This is especially valuable for Facebook, where hyperlinks can't be used.

Exploring Artificial Intelligence

Finally, **artificial intelligence (AI)** is revolutionizing the business landscape. While not a replacement for human involvement, AI can assist with various tasks. With basic input regarding your audience and desired messaging, AI tools can help generate social media posts, blog content, ad copy, handle your chat feature, and more. All business owners need to familiarize themselves with AI and explore how it can uniquely benefit their operations.

Conclusion

Technology can significantly enhance your business processes, improve customer engagement, and streamline operations. By incorporating these tools and approaches, you can foster growth, enhance efficiency, and set your small business up for long-term success.

Chapter 23

Maximizing Your Social Media Presence

When it comes to advertising, few quotes resonate as powerfully as that of John Wanamaker: **"Half the money I spend on advertising is wasted; the trouble is I don't know which half."** Effective advertising has always posed a challenge for businesses, big and small. However, with the rise of social media, we now have new opportunities to connect with potential customers—and new challenges to navigate.

Understanding Customer Engagement Points

The first step is determining which social media platforms will enable you to reach your target audience most effectively. This section will focus on Facebook. While other platforms offer visibility and possible access to prospective customers, Facebook is the most widely used for businesses. It's fastest-growing demographic is baby boomers, who currently hold about half of the wealth in the United States, making them an attractive audience for your message. If your product or service caters to a younger demographic, consider Instagram or TikTok as a platform.

1. **Contact Information Visibility**: Ensure that your social media pages clearly display essential information, including:

- Physical address
- Website URL
- Phone number
- Business hours

- An interactive map (if applicable)

This transparency helps prospective customers easily connect with you.

Harnessing the Power of Facebook

Facebook remains one of the most effective platforms for businesses. Here are some strategies to enhance your reach:

- **Post Consistently**: Develop a regular posting schedule. Many businesses start strong but drop off when they don't see immediate results. Avoid this pitfall by committing to consistent content sharing.

- **Balanced Content**: Limit direct sales pitches to about **25%** of your posts. Instead, share valuable content that engages your audience and encourages them to return to your page.

- **Grow Your Followers**: Increasing your follower count is essential for visibility. Consider these methods:

- **Invite Friends**: Use the "Invite Friends" feature to encourage your personal connections to follow your business page.

- **Engagement Invitations**: Invite those who engage with your posts to like your page. Click on the number of likes beneath your post to open a menu of those who have liked this particular post. You can click on the Invite button to follow or like your page.

- **Interact Regularly**: Respond to comments promptly. Thank people for their feedback and encourage them to ask questions. Active engagement increases your page's exposure on Facebook.

If you are using your personal Facebook page, consider converting it to a business page to view insights that will help you tune in the best-performing content for your followers. Use a CTA (call to action) button to encourage your customers to take the next step toward becoming a customer.

Post content that asks questions or polls followers for their thoughts and opinions. You will gain insight into what your followers like and don't like and expand your reach.

Ensure an icon and link to your Facebook page are on your website and other visible properties. With most providers, you can include it in your email signature.

Maintaining a Spam-Free Environment

Facebook faces constant challenges from spammers. Here's how to manage this issue:

- **Regularly Monitor Reviews**: Check your reviews frequently and promptly hide or delete any spammy comments or solicitations. This not only improves your page's appearance but also builds trust with genuine customers.

- **Country Restrictions**: Limit the visibility of your content to certain countries. Access your page settings and choose **Settings and Privacy > Settings > Followers and Public Content > Country Restrictions**. Reputable countries often maintain cleaner interactions. India, Nigeria, Pakistan, and China are known for high numbers of hackers, so if you don't sell there, blocking your content to those countries may be advantageous.

- **Comment Control**: Restrict who can comment on your posts. When posting, click the three dots in the top right corner of your post and select **"Who Can Comment on Your Post."** Limiting this to established followers minimizes spam and enhances the overall user experience.

Conclusion: Consistency and Engagement Matter

In today's world, a strong online presence is crucial. By being proactive in your social media strategy, you'll not only stand out but also stay relevant for years. Remember, it's not just about broadcasting your message; it's about building relationships, trust, and a sense of community around your brand.

Make the most of your social media channels by prioritizing customer engagement, actively managing your online presence, and continually refining your approach. Your efforts in maintaining a positive, informative, and engaging presence can lead to long-term business success.

Chapter 24

Understanding the Better Business Bureau

Few entities in the business world are as misunderstood as the Better Business Bureau (BBB). With a long history dating back to 1912, the BBB is a private, non-profit organization that serves both businesses and consumers. Its role, authority, and value often lead to misconceptions, but understanding the BBB can benefit your business significantly.

A Historical Perspective

Think of the BBB as the predecessor to modern review platforms like Google Reviews and Yelp. However, it's much more comprehensive. For years, the BBB served as the primary source of information about how businesses manage customer relations, uphold ethical standards, and respond to grievances.

Businesses are assigned grades based on their performance in handling complaints, transparency, ethical advertising, and other crucial criteria. These grades can serve as valuable research tools for prospective customers and act as a badge of honor for companies that excel.

Mediation and Transparency

Unlike typical online review sites, the BBB actively mediates customer concerns. Customers can leave reviews, but they also have the option to file formal complaints. Upon receiving a complaint, the BBB promptly contacts the business to ensure a balanced view of the issue. This mediation fosters transparency and encourages businesses to address customer concerns promptly.

While it's important to note that the BBB does not have the authority to take direct action against a company, it does publish any concerns alongside the business's response. This transparency allows potential customers to review a business's BBB profile and assess how responsive the company is to customer issues and complaints.

Services Offered by the BBB

The BBB provides a range of valuable mediation and arbitration services designed to help businesses resolve disputes without resorting to costly litigation. For more information, visit their website, where you can find resources tailored to your specific needs.

Membership Benefits

If you decide to become a BBB member, the cost will depend on your business size, specifically the number of employees. Membership not only grants you the right to display the BBB insignia both in your physical location and on your website but also signifies credibility to customers—especially those who associate the BBB with a standard of excellence.

While younger clients may not recognize the BBB's authority, many older consumers grew up viewing it as a gold standard for evaluating businesses. Displaying this credential can help build trust and enhance your reputation.

Showcasing Your Credibility

It's a good practice to showcase any industry-specific credentials on your website and social media platforms. Likewise, highlight any media coverage your business receives. Articles or segments featuring your business from independent media sources carry significant weight, offering credibility that self-promotion cannot achieve.

Conclusion

By understanding and utilizing the Better Business Bureau, small business owners can enhance their reputations, foster customer trust, and effectively address concerns. The BBB can be a powerful ally in your journey toward building a thriving business.

Chapter 25

Two Productive Tips from the Car Business

A "Save-A-Deal" Meeting

Many processes from the auto business could serve you well in yours. One is a save-a-deal meeting. It's an offshoot of the old adage that two heads are better than one. In this case, there would be several heads involved.

In these meetings, the sales and finance management teams get together and review the customers and deals worked from the previous day that weren't closed. Collectively they brainstorm as to ways the deal, or a deal, could possibly be made.

Knowing that we would always exhaust every effort to put a deal together while the customer was in the showroom, this session gives those who may have been off yesterday or busy with other deals a chance to offer a different perspective and fresh sets of eyes.

For example, we could have taken in a fresh trade-in later in the day, which would possibly be a perfect fit for that customer. If it's a question of getting financing approved, one manager may think of a vehicle that may work for the bank that the manager working the deal missed. We may have an option for a potentially higher bid for the customer's trade, which could help close the gap to making a deal. A new car with a big rebate to get the financed amount online for the bank is another potential suggestion. Occasionally, we'd realize that we had a retail prospect on the car the first customer was trading, and we find a way to make two deals.

T.O. (turnover)

A turnover is when a manager or more senior salesperson steps in when the original salesperson isn't looking like they are heading toward a sale. The person taking the turn can often identify what is needed to get the sale back on track. Sometimes, it's a matter of landing on the right product, unanswered objections or questions, or just making the prospective buyer feel more confident about purchasing.

Regardless of whether it makes a sale happen, a turnover gives managers/ owners great opportunities to get feedback about the customer's experience. It also is a chance to head off what could become a negative review by learning of and correcting any negatives in the customer's mind.

By and large, customers love having a manager or owner touching base. Doesn't it feel warm and welcoming when you've wrapped up a meal in a nice restaurant, and the owner or manager comes by, introduces themselves, asks you about your experience, and if there are any concerns or suggestions?

There's nothing but an upside to talking to customers in your business.

Section 4
Tips from Top Pros

125

Chapter 26

Banking for Small Businesses

Most business publications that have analyzed the failures of small businesses list a lack of capital and/or poor cash management as a primary reason for shutting down. It is a difficult hurdle to overcome if your new venture is undercapitalized from the onset. Still, that challenge becomes greater if the assets are not managed as effectively as possible.

It is impossible to overstate the importance of a business owner's relationship with their banker. Many only reach out to their most important contact when they need help, and often at the last minute. To help our readers get a clear picture of the relationship from the banker's side and a look at what they need on their end to better help their small business clients, we reached out to an expert in the field. Mike Kramer has an extensive resumé in the financial industry and has provided valuable insights that can help you solidify your banking connections and better manage your capital.

Introduction

I am a retired banker who, over a thirty-five-year banking career, led four public company banks as either COO or CEO. We built robust banking businesses focused on small businesses, their owners, and principals in all four banks I led. We had some success and learned many lessons along the way. In this chapter, I'll attempt to provide an overview of how small businesses, including non-profits, have dealt most successfully with financial institutions. I've used the terms banks, thrifts, and credit unions; at other times, I've used the term financial institutions to describe these institutions. Most of what I am sharing is from my experience and the experience of other bankers like myself. I've included a handful of sources for material I've quoted or otherwise referenced at the end of this chapter. Working with your banker does not need to be a mystery; they typically make rational decisions. However, like most people, they make decisions for their reasons, not yours. Understanding their priorities, the "hows," and most importantly, the "whys" behind how they think is critical to a successful relationship with your financial institution.

The Basic Functions of Banks, Thrifts, and Credit Unions

Three major types of depository institutions exist: commercial banks, thrifts (which include savings and loan associations and savings banks), and credit unions.

These three types of institutions have become more like each other in recent decades, and their unique identities have become less distinct. However, they still differ in specialization, emphasis, and regulatory and supervisory structures.

Commercial Banks

Commercial banks are the traditional "department stores" of the financial services world; they receive deposits and hold them in various accounts, extend credit through loans and other instruments, and facilitate the movement of funds. While commercial banks mainly specialize in short-term business credit, they also make consumer loans and mortgages and have a broad range of financial products beyond essential credit and deposit products, including Treasury Management, Payment Processing, Investment Management, Trust Administration, and many others.

Savings and Loans/Savings Banks

Savings, loan associations, and savings banks specialize in real estate lending, particularly for single-family homes and other residential properties. These institutions are called "thrifts" because they initially offered only savings accounts or time deposits. Over the last twenty-five years, they have acquired a wide range of financial powers, and now many are indistinguishable from commercial banks. In the early 1990s, the supervision of federally chartered thrifts was transferred to the Office of the Comptroller of the Currency. Since then, Thrifts have been given all the same powers as commercial banks, and now, many are indistinguishable from their commercial banking competitors.

Credit Unions

Credit unions were originally formed as cooperative financial institutions by groups of people with a "common bond." Membership in a credit union was not open to the general public but was restricted to people who shared the common bond of the group that created the credit union. Over the last thirty years, "Community or Corporate Credit Unions" have been established to serve all people, including small businesses in a particular geography. They operate as non-profit institutions that seek to encourage savings and make excess funds within a community available at low cost to their members.

Credit unions accept deposits in a variety of accounts. All credit unions offer savings accounts or time deposits; most also offer checking and money market accounts. Credit unions' financial powers have expanded to include almost anything a bank or savings association can do, including making home loans, issuing credit cards, and even commercial loans. Credit unions are exempt from federal taxation.

Risk Management

Risk management in financial institutions involves identifying, assessing, and mitigating potential risks to ensure financial stability. Basic functions include credit risk assessment, market risk analysis, operational risk management, and liquidity risk monitoring. Banks also engage in stress testing, compliance with regulations, and developing contingency plans to navigate unforeseen challenges. The goal is to balance risk and reward while safeguarding the institution and its stakeholders.

The Role of the Regulators

Regulators play a crucial role in banking by overseeing and enforcing rules to ensure the stability and integrity of the financial system. They establish and enforce regulations to safeguard depositors, maintain fair competition, and prevent financial crimes. Regulators also monitor banks' capital adequacy, risk management practices, and compliance with legal and ethical standards. By supervising institutions, regulators aim to foster public confidence, promote financial stability, and mitigate systemic risks within the banking sector. Regulatory compliance has become increasingly complex over the last 25 years, going far beyond the efforts to ensure safety and soundness. Following the 911 attacks, Congress passed the Patriot Act, which requires banks to monitor accounts for potential links to terrorists. Similarly, Congress passed the Sarbanes Oxley Act following the Enron meltdown, requiring public company banks to attest to the quality and adequacy of their internal audit and overall financial statement control environment. Legislation such as these adds thousands of hours of paperwork, millions of dollars in compliance costs, and added disclosure rules for clients, increasing the complexity of dealing with financial institutions.

Public, Private, and Mutual Ownership

Public ownership refers to banks owned by the public through the stock market. Private ownership implies ownership by an individual or a small group of individuals without a ready market for those shares. Mutual ownership involves shared ownership by the bank's customers or members. Each type has distinct governance structures and implications for decision-making and profit distribution. Typically, the pressure for high earnings is greatest in publicly owned banking companies and lowest in mutuals and credit unions.

How Financial Institutions make money and why that matters to your organization

If you've watched "It's a Wonderful Life," the Christmas classic starring Jimmy Stewart as George Bailey, the Manager of the local Building & Loan (a "Thrift"), you've seen an accurate and excellent explanation of how Financial Institutions make money. During a run on the bank, Bailey explains to his customers attempting to withdraw all their deposits that their money isn't held at the bank. It is invested in their neighbor's homes and businesses. If you've never seen this, it is worth watching:

https://www.youtube.com/watch?v=iPkJH6BT7dM

Banks make money primarily by investing customer deposits in loans or purchasing securities and bonds. The deposits they collect are used to make loans to individuals and businesses. The interest rate they charge for loans is typically higher than the interest rate they pay on deposits. Fees for services such as account maintenance charges and debit card transaction fees (both consumer and merchant fees) contribute to their revenue. Banks also generate income by investing in financial instruments such as Municipal, Treasury, and Mortgage-Backed bonds, securities, and other assets. Larger financial institutions often have mortgage divisions that generate fees from the origination and sale of mortgage loans, Trust & Wealth Management Divisions that generate revenue from the management of client investments and the administration of Trusts and Treasury Management divisions that generate fees from cash management, merchant services, and payment processing.

Community banks, thrifts, and credit unions typically generate approximately 60-70% of their net income from net interest margin (the difference between what they pay for deposits versus what they charge for loans). Large banks with various fee income generation opportunities generate 40 -50% of their net income from net interest margin. The implication for your organization is that larger banks can typically offer more competitive interest rates because their net income is less reliant on net interest margin. Credit unions also depend on net interest margin for income, but because they pay no federal or state income taxes (unlike banks and mutuals), they can offer higher deposits and lower loan rates than the typical community bank. Community banks work hard to mitigate these pricing differences through higher levels of personalized service. The most recent JD Power Customer Satisfaction surveys support this contention; Community Banks ranked first in ten of the fourteen regions measured for Client Service satisfaction.

Understanding your needs from your Banker's Perspective

Knowing how your banker views the relationship is helpful when considering your working relationship with a financial institution.

Let's start with your deposit relationship; a good banker will evaluate the following fact pattern as it relates to your deposit accounts:

What is the average balance in your account(s) held at the financial institution?

- The amount of cash that runs through your account is not as significant as the amount that stays in the account because this is the amount on which the bank can make investments and loans.

Transactions (deposits and withdrawals) are much less important than the average balance, even if fees are associated with them.

- This ties back to the reality that 60-70% of the typical bank's income is tied to net interest margin, and margin is measured by the difference between what banks charge their customers for loans and what they pay their customers for deposits. Consequently, a higher average balance in a deposit account is worth more to the bank than a low balance.

What other deposit services is your company using?

- Remote Deposit Capture – the image capture of checks taken for payment and digital transfer of that image to the bank (replaces going to the bank to make a deposit) – typically associated with higher volumes of checks

- Mobile Deposit – the same as Remote Deposit Capture but for smaller volumes of checks

- Merchant Processing – the processing associated with accepting credit cards and other forms of cashless payments

- Purchasing Cards – Credit/Debit Cards issued to replace the use of checks for purchases

These "other deposit services" all generate income and often eliminate expenses for the financial institution; understanding this (whether your banker does or not) can help as you navigate your relationship with a bank. As an example, if you are working to negotiate a more competitive loan rate, understanding that your use of the bank for merchant processing is generating income for the financial institution and your use of remote deposit capture or mobile deposit is saving the bank money can be used to help convince the bank a lower rate or better terms in their best interest as well as yours.

When analyzing your credit-worthiness a bank will consider several factors:

Your capital, the paid-in-capital or retained earnings, and cash reserves

- Paid-in-Capital is the amount of money you and/or your partners initially invested in the business

- Retained earnings are the earnings the company has generated that have not been distributed to the owner(s)

- Cash Reserve is the amount of cash you have in the bank, thrift, or credit union

  Your recurring, predictable revenues and income

- Your earnings and revenues for the last two to three years and the trend that represents

The amount of debt requested and the ability of your recurring, predictable income to service the debt (paying back principle and interest according to the terms) without impairing your overall financial condition.

- If your organization is generating roughly $15,000 per month in net income and needs to borrow $500,000 over seven years, the monthly payment (at 8% interest) will be $7,800.

- The banker will want to determine how this payment impacts your organization's cash flows.

If a credit request is for expansion, the financial institution will attempt to estimate the amount of realized new revenue or cost savings the expansion will create, and the organization will realize

The stability of your leadership team, Board, and client base

- How long have you been in business, how long have key employees been with you, and who are your clients are all questions a good banker will examine

Revenue concentration – is your organization dependent on one or a small group of clients for a large (over 35%) portion of your revenue? If so, the bank will attempt to evaluate the stability of that relationship.

Board Governance and why it matters to your Banking relationship

If your company or organization has a governing or advisory Board, it can be beneficial to highlight their role in your organization for a banker. Proactively addressing the composition of your Board regarding financial, governance, and revenue creation expertise and their connection to your markets and community is helpful for a banker to assess the stability and professionalism of your organization.

If you have a Board or decide to add one, consider including these reporting functions:

Financials: Your Board should be reviewing the financial performance of your company regularly, no less than quarterly, and if you are in a fast growth mode or struggling, more often, perhaps monthly. If you have a governing Board, a Finance or Audit Committee should regularly review financial performance and an annual audit by a qualified Public Accounting firm. The advisor or Committee should be comprised of financial professionals who understand the organization's Balance Sheet and Income Statements and are familiar with the work of an auditor (if required).

HR/Compensation: Human Resource issues and legal compliance with labor laws and protections have grown evermore complicated. Navigating these rules often requires more skill than a small business or non-profit can afford. Adding an HR professional to your group of advisors or forming a Committee of leaders who deal with HR issues can augment your team and your knowledge much more efficiently than turning to a labor lawyer or consultant at every turn. These advisors or committee members can be particularly valuable in understanding market practices and opportunities in the compensation arena. Knowing the standard market practices around compensation practices and trends can positively impact turnover and effectively manage labor costs with actual data rather than just guessing.

Advancement/Sales & Marketing: whether it's called fund-raising for the non-profit or revenue generation for the small business, the goal is the same: how do you increase revenue for the entity? A committee or an advisor who brings these skills and experience to the table is critical to advancing the organization.

Governance: this is mostly for governing boards. A Governance committee typically does two things: understand and help management accurately apply the Operating Agreement or Bylaws of the organization and work to identify and nominate needed Board members to perpetuate the entity's work.

If you do not require a governing board and do not have an advisory board, consider adding a small group of seasoned professionals as an advisory board to your company. The advice of a banker, lawyer, accountant, and sales/marketing leaders who are paid a nominal board fee (many will serve for $250 - $500 / quarter) should prove invaluable.

How to find your banking "fit"

In discussing your needs from the banker's perspective, we highlighted the fact patterns bankers look for: the characteristics of your deposit relationship and your credit needs. Before seeking out a banker, take the time to do some "self-analysis." Ask and answer the following questions:

Is your business growing quickly? Will you need to borrow money to expand your operation, add capacity, hire additional staff, or purchase new equipment, or can you fund these needs out of generated cash?

1. Determining whether you'll need to borrow to fund these needs or can fund out of generated cash isn't a complex equation. Estimating the amount of cash you have on hand and how much net cash (net cash earnings) your organization will generate over the next relevant period versus the investment required and the impact on remaining cash can help you determine whether it is prudent to borrow or self-fund.

2. There is a difference between debt and leverage – many advisors are against debt in any form, and too much debt is one of the

primary reasons small businesses fail. According to SCORE, 82% of small businesses fail due to cash flow problems, and if you dig deeper, there is often too much debt to service, leading to cash problems.

3. Too much debt, particularly long-term debt, can limit your ability to operate optimally. Leverage is the capital you borrow to grow your enterprise, not to start it, maintain it, or grow it. The growth the leverage is expected to help generate should make it possible to pay the debt back quickly without negatively impacting cash flow.

4. If the need to borrow to fund your next round of expansion describes your organization, you should be speaking with bankers who focus   on lending to small businesses.

5. Banks with government-guaranteed lending functions loans guaranteed by the SBA or the USDA can be attractive under certain circumstances, which I'll discuss further in this chapter.

6. If the ability to fund your expansion lies in your ability to generate cash, you should seek financial institutions known for their Treasury, Cash Management, and Payment processing expertise.

7. These two are not mutually exclusive and can be found in the same institution with some research and help from the right advisors. Your accountant and the local Chamber of Commerce are great places to start this process if you don't have a Board or group of advisors.

Best Practices – Treasury Management

Is your cash working for you? When writing this, most financial institutions pay north of 4.5% on Money Market Accounts ("MMA"), some as high as 5.5%. A balance of $1M would generate $55,000 in annual interest income. Have you reviewed how much excess cash you keep in your operating account? A conversation with your banker, accountant, or financial advisor about an appropriate amount of cash in your operating account versus total operating cash can be revealing. The US Chamber of Commerce recommends that small businesses maintain three to six months of operating cash in reserve; my advice to small business owners over the years has mirrored this but goes further: consider managing your operating cash through sweep products. Most banks can set up a "sweep" account that manages your operating account cash down to nearly zero, transferring funds back and forth, as needed, between the operating account and either an investment or money market account. As mentioned earlier, MMA rates in the high fours to mid-five percent range can generate positive returns on your excess cash with little risk.

A Story to illustrate: Years ago, my bank won the business of a small glass bottle manufacturer. This client's business worked primarily with distillers to provide engraved and labeled bottles. The business generated significant cash, mostly sitting in an operating account. In this case, the company was generating roughly $90,000 per month after tax in excess cash. Monthly, the bookkeeper would transfer extra cash to a Money Market Account, earning below-market returns. When the business billed their clients, they typically received payment within 30 days, receiving checks as payment. Our bank won the business by offering several ideas to increase cash flow and to make their excess cash generate income. First, we offered a daily sweep account that transferred excess cash every night into a Money Market paying market rates. We also set the client up with the ability to accept credit cards from their clients; we knew through other relationships that many large distillers were comfortable paying their invoices with a Purchasing Card. This increased the speed of payment, provided material additional interest income, and saved the bookkeeper time by eliminating the monthly transfer.

Best Practices - POS Systems

What are you doing to accelerate the speed with which payments you receive are accounted for in your operating account? Point of Sale technologies ("POS") have advanced tremendously over the last few years. POS systems that accept typical payments such as Credit/Debit cards have advanced to accept Apple Pay, Venmo, Paypal, Zelle, etc. These cashless payments can often be credited to your account faster than cards and with lower return and decline rates. A quick search on POS systems turns up several highly recommended vendors. Scheduling a demo can usually be done online.

POS systems have evolved to do much more than process cards. Some of the features associated with modern POS systems:

Inventory Management: POS systems can link your inventory tracking to purchases, notify you when inventories are low, and be configured to order replacement inventory automatically. They can also report what is selling and what isn't to help determine customer preferences.

eCommerce: POS systems can be linked to your online sales efforts, capturing detailed client contact data for ongoing client communication

Customer Relationship Management: POS systems can be used to capture and track client data, including purchase preferences, frequency, online versus in-person visits, and more

Appointment/Reservations Scheduling: businesses such as spas, salons, and restaurants that require this feature can find them in some POS systems, and many POS systems link to reservations system providers

Loyalty Programs: Some POS systems can generate purchase tracking data to provide loyalty rewards offerings

Scheduling: Some POS providers bundle HR, Payroll, and Scheduling platforms with their Point of Sale platforms.

Results Reporting: many POS platforms provide real-time data reporting on client visits and sales volumes, revenue, and labor costs (hours worked and labor rates).

Reviewing these systems, setting up demonstrations, and talking with peers and other users can be a lot of work, but it is work that can pay enormous dividends in efficiency for the daily job of running your business.

A Story to illustrate: Years ago, our bank worked with a client who owned a chain of high-end car washes. These were fully automated car washes that featured various levels of service. We won the business on the strength of our credit products that helped finance the expansion of multiple locations. One factor in our assessment was the data that this client used to manage his business. His POS system provided real-time tracking of throughput in each of his locations (client visits and associated revenue). The systems were integrated into his labor scheduling and payroll system; consequently, he could determine if any location was overstaffed or understaffed in relation to how busy the location was and could expect to be. This client's command of the information driving his business (volumes, revenue, labor expense) impressed our underwriting team to be more aggressive on our rates and terms to win the business.

Best Practices – Debt/Liquidity Management

Liquidity management refers to optimizing a company's ability to meet its short-term financial obligations while maintaining sufficient cash reserves.

Effective liquidity management includes:

Cash flow forecasting: Predicting future cash inflows and outflows to anticipate potential liquidity needs and plan accordingly.

Cash reserves: Maintaining adequate cash reserves or liquidity buffers to cover unexpected expenses or temporary cash shortfalls.

- Establishing credit lines can provide access to additional liquidity when needed.

Monitoring and analysis: Regularly monitoring cash flow patterns, liquidity ratios, and other financial metrics to identify potential risks or opportunities for improvement.

- Reviewing your total debt service requirements and assessing if the rates and terms you've agreed to represent fair market value can be the first step towards possibly negotiating better terms and rates

It's understandable if this sounds like the work of a highly trained CFO that your organization can't afford. Fortunately for small businesses, technology solutions can provide the monitoring and forecasting that effective debt/liquidity management requires. Systems like upSWOT, Monit, Prime Dash, and Boss Insights can link to your accounting systems (Quickbooks, NetSuite, etc.) and your bank(s) to provide cash flow analysis and forecasting.

A Story to illustrate: A start-up business whose governing Board I serve on was struggling to find a CFO candidate who could manage through the complexity of the company's financials was proving to be complicated. The role was equal parts operational and financial; however, the operational side required far more attention. Having reviewed multiple tech platforms, one of the company's banks utilized upSWOT for its small business clients. The company used upSWOT to deliver cash flow reporting, monitoring, and forecasting until hiring a CFO. upSWOT, easily integrated with all of the company's banks, accounting, and POS systems to deliver a full view of the company's long-term debt service performance, short-term debt availability, available cash, projected available cash and projections around the potential need to use the company's line of credit (short-term debt availability). This platform was instrumental in helping the company bridge to hire a full-time CFO and assisted the eventual hire as she ramped up to full competency in the role. Although a start-up, this company generates several million dollars in monthly revenues, serving consumers exclusively through web portals, resulting in a complex operating platform. These modern technology platforms can easily integrate with the most complicated situations; imagine their impact on a less complex business.

Best Practices – Know Your Banker

Many small businesses make the mistake of only calling the bank or their banker when they need something. You are indeed the client, and a good banker shouldn't wait to hear from you. Unfortunately, bankers are human and subject to the old rule; "the squeaky wheel gets the grease." Take the initiative and get to know the bank and the banker serving as your relationship manager. Ask questions such as:

What are your bank's highest priorities right now?

Who is the best competitor you face every day? What makes them so good?

Who do you think is our company's best competitor? Why?

What are some of the best practices in companies/organizations like ours?

Have you reviewed our financials? Do you see any trends we should discuss?

What's the most interesting technology you see other companies our size deploying? How are they using it?

My late father was fond of saying, "Good things come to those who ask." In this situation, I'd apply it by suggesting that you meet other bankers and explore banking alternatives, especially if everything is going well. The best time to examine your financial options is when you don't have to. Finding an alternative when things are difficult is exponentially more challenging. If you don't know where to start, trust your advisors, accountants, lawyers, board members, peers, and friendly competitors.

A Story to Illustrate: Early in my tenure at the last bank I led, we asked all of our commercial and business bankers to present their five largest clients to the new leadership team we had assembled. Each banker was asked to provide an overview of the business, its ownership structure, the products and services it offered, and the company's leadership. We also asked for a review of the company's financial performance and balance sheet (cash, non-cash assets such as equipment, inventory or real estate, debt, and capital). Lastly, each banker was asked to present an analysis of the client's strengths, weaknesses, most significant opportunities, and threats – a classic SWOT analysis. One of the clients presented that day evidenced strong cash flow, a strong balance sheet, and a history of paying the bank back on time, as expected. When it came time to discuss the SWOT analysis, a fact pattern emerged that every project we had been involved in with this client resulted in the client engaging in litigation. His business or he, sometimes both, were sued or suing another person or entity in every engagement; our banker described it as "that's how he does business." To be fair, our bank had never been named in any of these suits, so we had little to no litigation risk; however, this led to increased complexity in his business and our dealings. Ultimately, we decided to end our relationship with this client and asked him to begin the process of moving his relationship to another financial institution. When asked why we were taking this step, I explained that "there are many banks and many clients, not every bank is right for every client, and not every client is right for every bank. While we appreciated that he had paid us as agreed, the level of complexity in his business, due to the constancy of litigation, wasn't "right" for our bank.

We worked with this client for over six months to help him move his accounts to other financial institutions. We attempted to be cooperative and supportive but firm in our conviction that the accounts would leave. Fortunately for this client, he knew other banks and bankers, which made this process much easier than it could have been. Banks and bankers change all the time – know your alternatives.

Conclusion

If I had to limit my advice for small business owners to one thing, it would be this: surround yourself with a robust group of advisors. Whether that is a governing or advisory board, populate it with experts in those areas of the business you are not an expert in. Leading an organization is complex; you cannot be expected to know everything, and there are not enough hours in the day to adequately research every idea included in these pages. Advisors can help you explore new technologies, solve HR issues, learn which bank works best with small organizations, and so much more. The key to finding that advisor group? Good things come to those who ask!

Sources

https://www.kansascityfed.org/Economic%20Review/documents/8634/EconomicReviewV107N1SenguptaXue.pdf

https://www.jdpower.com/business/press-releases/2022-us-retail-banking-satisfaction-study

https://www.score.org/resource/blog-post/1-reason-small-businesses-fail-and-how-avoid-it

https://www.uschamber.com/co/run/finance/cash-on-hand-considerations-for-businesses#:~:text=As%20a%20general%20rule%20of,whatever%20amount%20you%20set%20aside

https://www.forbes.com/advisor/l/best-pos-systems/

Chapter 27

Facility Leasing

It's easy to think of your location as little more than a necessary expense to provide you and your business with a place to operate and sell your goods and/or services. For many first-time lessees, the process can make buying a car or house look like child's play. There are many aspects that, if not addressed up front, may have effects that linger for years.

When Marian and I operated our fitness businesses in North Georgia, all of our facilities were leased. Our first location was a basement beneath a landscape office, and we expanded to multiple locations of all shapes and sizes. The situations we encountered provided us with a wide range of experiences, some costly and a couple that severely impacted our ability to sustain ourselves.

Our first fitness business was a personal training studio that, over time, became specialized in working with high-risk individuals. Our clients were working to overcome trauma like paralysis, spinal injuries from serious accidents, detached tendons and muscles, and diseases like MS and cancer. Working with these high-risk folks could easily become dangerous with even the slightest distraction, so a quiet environment was essential.

As to all leases in the state where we operated, there was a provision for quiet enjoyment. Using the advice of a friend in place of seeking legal counsel prior to signing the lease, we were told that meant we had the right to quiet use of our space. In other words, our neighbors had to be quiet, and so did we. Or so we thought.

What we found out that what really means is that a landlord has no right to deny you access to your leased facility provided you are not in default of the lease. It has nothing to do with your neighbors "disturbing your peace." We had to relocate twice because of this exact reason.

A fair question would be how we didn't learn a lesson from the first relocation. We did and addressed it in our second lease. Shortly after we moved in, the property was sold, and the new owners began a massive and lengthy remodeling project, which was very disruptive to our clients and their safety. Once again, we relocated. From then on, we made sure it was included very specifically in the lease contracts and never had that issue arise again.

An issue with another location involved parking and the neighboring tenants living up to their responsibilities. The spaces available for our business were too few for the size of the business, but the owner we purchased the business from had an arrangement with a convenience store next door to have access to about twenty spaces, which made our model workable.

Before closing on the lease, we visited the neighboring store's owners to make sure that our arrangement would continue after we took over. We were assured that it would, as it was beneficial to the store as well. Many of our members visited the store to purchase drinks, snacks, etc.

Several months after we moved in, however, I received a letter from a real estate management firm advising us that we would no longer have access to those spaces. When I responded that we had an agreement with the store owner, I was shocked to discover that the spaces in question were not a part of the store's property but part of a strip center that also bordered our line. They gave us a month to make other arrangements and offered us a rental for a dozen spaces that were 250 feet further away and often standing in a foot or so of water from poor drainage.

In a third incident, the property we were leasing was adjacent to a phone store. Because the center's handicapped spaces were in front of our door, our lease came with two parking spaces that were clearly marked as for our customers only and were presented as a major value in our arrangement.

This was ignored by the phone store and its customers, who parked in our reserved spaces freely, rendering the value of the spaces included in our lease as nil. Negligence on the part of the phone store's employees also resulted in water damage to drywall and carpeting. Other tenants ignored provisions in each of our leases about tacky and unprofessional marketing material, window ads, etc. In each case, the landlord would do absolutely nothing to enforce the standards or protect our property and interests.

The lessons from each of these experiences could serve us all well. Get everything discussed and important to you included in the lease with very specific verbiage. A year into the lease is too late to do anything.

To offer more insight and help about this crucial component of your business, I've reached out to a top industry professional and asked for his advice, in the form of tips, from new lessees.

L. Max Lehmann is a 45-year veteran of the Atlanta Commercial Real Estate market with a vast array of experience in both sides of leasing. His advice follows.

Should you hire a commercial real estate agent if you are looking to open a small business?

First, if you are contemplating hanging a sign out as a small business owner, congratulations and heartfelt wishes for your best success! Small business ownership is virtually the toughest and most rewarding work you'll ever do.

"Why work 40 hours a week for someone else when you can work 80 hours for yourself?"

Many small businesses evolve from a place in the residence to a storage unit, to a leased facility. Sometimes the business genesis is a direct leasehold because the owner was 'downsized' from their longtime corporate gig – Whatever the circumstances, all cases have their nexus on Location, Location, Location.

I was asked to write a few words on how to do this, and frankly, there is so much written on the topic I am going to try to make this concise, relevant, and useful. First off, do you want to handle the intricacies of a commercial lease yourself or be represented by an Commercial Real Estate Agent (CRE)?

By way of anecdote, here is my somewhat biased answer. I built a sweet garden shed and went to a popular garage door manufacturer to buy a roll-up door. I asked if the documentation was good, and can I install it myself. "It'll probably come out better the next time," was the answer given. I paid the installation fee and never gave the matter a second thought.

Even a 1,000 square foot (SF) lease represents a relatively high-dollar contract. You would be wise to have an attorney review the lease. But the lawyer won't negotiate business terms, conditions, and rental rates, instead, they will make sure the legal language is not overly onerous or unenforceable in Court.

I spent time researching how to hire a good commercial agent, so those tips are out there. Sticking to my plan, here are some concise tips on hiring an Agent:

Where are you going to set up shop? Smaller, rural communities often lack a dedicated CRE, in fact, you may know the Landlord (LL). In those cases, make sure to read ahead to Major Lease Considerations below. In a larger market, choosing an Agent should be likened to having a relationship with a seasoned businessperson who can provide a wide range of strategic business assistance beyond the initial lease. A good CRE Agent knows they will be paid upon a lease renewal if they participate in negotiating that event, if needed. Therefore, your Agent has a reason to be in touch with you quarterly. That can be useful over a multi-year period.

Why do I need a CRE Agent? Other than the garage door example, the CRE Agent fee is already baked into the lease rate. You won't get a discount for not being represented and the LL Agent doesn't represent you. The LL Agent must be legally honest, but they don't negotiate against the LL; your Agent should do that. In fact, most LL Agents prefer to speak Agent-to-Agent because there may be a trust factor (Known prior quality deals) and it is faster.

Major Lease Considerations: Retail, Office, Industrial are all uniquely drafted.

Personal Guarantee:

As a start-up, the LL needs to be sold on you, your business, and the deal, in that order. LL's must own up to owners why a lease turned out poorly, so that uncomfortable conversation may lead to an end of their Agency with the LL.

In other words, the Personal Guarantee is almost always going to be a part of your first lease. Sadly, the Personal Guarantee makes you personally liable for the remaining lease amount, plus fees, charges, etc. It is universally despised by Tenants for good reason. They can take your stuff and your sparkly, new LLC doesn't shield you from it.

Here is what is needed to avoid a personal guarantee:

Well capitalized and have a verifiable multi-year business track record, a solid business plan with sales tax receipts, two prior years of tax records, and quantifiable accounting records, plus solid banking and commercial references. In other words, you probably are NOT a start-up!

Sometimes, the Personal Guarantee can be negotiated to burn-off if all lease terms and rents are in order. That is a delicate and nuanced conversation to sell to a LL.

Tenant Improvements: TIs

The best way to summarize is that anything LL has to do to earn your business is negotiable. If you are a strong Tenant and the market is soft, TIs are more generous; the opposite is true with a start-up and a weak market.

Retail:

Typically, retail space is offered to the Tenant as a "vanilla shell" which means an empty, clean, buildable space. Most leases require you to return the space in that condition, though that is negotiable. So, be cautious about spending your capital on TI's. You may need that money to capitalize your fledging business.

Office: Less is More

The best fit for an office is one that requires the least amount of TI's. LL is more willing to negotiate a rental concession if you are able to take the space 'as-is.' New paint and carpet are a good starting point, but if the existing space is workable, you may wish to forego that in lieu of a lower rental rate.

Industrial:

The warehouse should have the necessary loading arrangement for your needs, though dock doors can be ramped if you need another drive-in door. That's not inexpensive, so it is best to find what you need instead.

The office area follows the same guidelines as above.

Critical Terms:

Who has control of the leasehold at the end of the lease? This is one of the most important lease terms, and it is rarely negotiated. Assuming the best and you're very successful, what happens in three to five years? Landlords are often encouraged when they see a new business offering to extend their lease. This benefits you because you are setting the lease rate and terms instead of renewing at 'then-current' market rates.

Each type of lease, Retail, Office, and Industrial may be written differently, with different types of terms. This Primer cannot address these detailed legal terms adequately; just know that a CRE can make this process easier to navigate while you run your business.

With the internet and enough time, you can learn the critical 'negotiating points' of any type of lease. The question is, "Will you do it better the next time?" A small oversight can be very costly.

153

Chapter 28

Tax Tips

Several dilemmas confront small business owners, and two of the big ones involve accounting. One of the majors is the balance between showing the lowest possible profit, in compliance with the current tax code, but knowing that you also need a strong P&L for your bank, should you need loans. Along those same lines, you want to lower your tax liability to the smallest amount possible yet be covered in the case of an audit. Penalties and interest from our friends at the IRS can make a major dink in your bank balance and can often make the difference in survival and closing.

For advice along these lines, we contacted an expert, Sara Poe. Sara is a Certified Public Accountant and graciously provided these tips for you.

Sara-

There are several common tax deductions that small businesses can take advantage of. It's important to keep detailed records and receipts for all expenses you plan to deduct. Never co-mingle personal and business expenses. Additionally, it's recommended to consult with a tax professional or accountant to ensure you are correctly applying the tax deductions that are applicable to your business and complying with all relevant tax laws and regulations.

1. **Business Expenses:** This includes deductions for ordinary and necessary expenses directly related to your business operations. Examples may include rent, utilities, office supplies, equipment, and professional services.

2. **Home Office Deduction**: If you use a portion of your home exclusively for your business, you may be eligible to deduct related expenses such as a portion of your rent or mortgage interest, property taxes, utilities, and insurance.

3. **Vehicle Expenses**: If you use a vehicle for business purposes, you can typically deduct expenses such as fuel, maintenance, insurance, and depreciation. You have the option to choose between the standard mileage rate or the actual expense method.

4. **Travel and Entertainment:** Expenses incurred while traveling for business purposes, such as airfare, accommodations, meals, and transportation, may be deductible. Additionally, you may be able to deduct a portion of entertainment expenses that are directly related to your business activities.

5. **Employee Wages and Benefits:** Wages, salaries, bonuses, and benefits paid to employees, including health insurance premiums, retirement contributions, and paid leave, are generally deductible expenses for small businesses.

6. **Self-Employment Taxes:** If you are self-employed, you can deduct the employer portion of self- employment taxes, such as Social Security and Medicare taxes.

7. **Professional Services:** Fees paid to professionals such as accountants, attorneys, and consultants for services related to your business are generally deductible.

8. **Advertising and Marketing:** Expenses for advertising and promoting your business, including website costs, online ads, print ads, and business cards, are typically deductible.

9. **Education and Training:** Costs associated with continuing education, professional development courses, and industry conferences that are relevant to your business may be deductible.

10. **Bad Debts:** If you have uncollectible accounts receivable or unpaid invoices, you may be able to deduct them as bad debts.

11. **Depreciation:** You can deduct the cost of business assets, such as machinery, equipment, and vehicles, over their useful lifespan through depreciation. There are various methods to calculate depreciation, including the Modified Accelerated Cost Recovery System (MACRS).

12. **Rent:** If you lease office space, a retail store, or any other business premises, the rent payments are generally deductible. This also includes equipment or machinery you lease for your business operations.

13. **Insurance Premiums:** Premiums paid for business insurance policies, including general liability insurance, professional liability insurance, property insurance, and business interruption insurance, are deductible expenses.

14. **Retirement Contributions:** Contributions made to retirement plans, such as Simplified Employee Pension (SEP) IRA or a solo 401(k) plan, are generally tax-deductible for the business.

15. **Software and Subscriptions:** Expenses for business software, such as accounting software, productivity tools, and industry-specific software, can be deducted. Additionally, subscriptions to business-related publications, trade magazines, or online services may also be deductible.

16. **Charitable Contributions:** If your business makes donations to qualified charitable organizations, those contributions may be

deductible. However, there are specific rules and limitations for deducting charitable contributions, so it's important to follow the guidelines set by the tax authorities.

17. **Licenses and Permits:** Fees paid for business licenses, permits, and registrations required to operate your business are generally deductible.

18. **Repairs and Maintenance:** Expenses for routine repairs and maintenance of business property, equipment, and vehicles can be deductible. However, improvements that add value or extend the useful life of the asset typically need to be capitalized and depreciated.

19. **Telephone and Internet Expenses:** Business-related telephone and internet expenses, including monthly service fees, may be deductible. If you use these services for both personal and business purposes, you can only deduct the portion that relates to your business activities.

20. **Bank Fees and Interest:** Fees paid for bank accounts, credit card processing, and business loans, as well as interest on business loans and business credit cards, can generally be deducted.

21. **Start-up Expenses:** If you recently started your business, you may be able to deduct certain costs associated with starting up, such as market research, advertising, professional fees, and employee training. There are specific rules and limitations for deducting start-up expenses, so it's advisable to consult a tax professional.

22. **Health Insurance Premiums:** If you are self-employed and pay for your own health insurance, you may be eligible to deduct the premiums you pay for yourself, your spouse, and your

dependents. There are certain criteria that must be met, so it's important to review the guidelines provided by the tax authorities.

23. **Education and Training for Employees:** Expenses for training and education programs provided to your employees can be deductible. This includes workshops, seminars, and courses that enhance their skills and knowledge relevant to their job duties.

24. **Research and Development (R&D) Expenses:** If your business is engaged in qualified research and development activities, you may be eligible for tax credits or deductions related to those expenses. R&D tax incentives can vary by country, so it's important to understand the specific regulations in your jurisdiction.

25. **State and Local Taxes:** In addition to federal taxes, small businesses may be eligible to deduct state and local taxes, such as income taxes or sales taxes paid on business-related purchases.

26. **Disaster and Theft Losses:** If your business experiences losses due to a natural disaster, fire, or theft, you may be able to deduct the unrecovered portion of those losses. There are specific rules and requirements for claiming these deductions, so it's important to consult with a tax professional.

27. **Legal and Professional Fees:** Fees paid to attorneys, accountants, and other professionals for business-related services can generally be deducted. This includes fees for tax preparation, legal advice, and consulting services.

28. **Environmental Deductions:** Some businesses may be eligible for deductions related to environmentally friendly activities or investments, such as energy-efficient upgrades or renewable

energy systems. These deductions are often aimed at promoting sustainability and reducing environmental impact.

Chapter 29

Social Media

Effective advertising has always been a challenge for businesses, small and large. As you read in an earlier chapter, successful 1800s businessman John Wanamaker once famously said, "Half the money I spend on advertising is wasted; the trouble is I don't know which half."

It is an inexact science, without a doubt. No matter what you are selling, it is unlikely that you can reach every prospective buyer for that good or service, and chances are, you'll spend a lot reaching people who are not prospective buyers.

In the late 1990s, our dealerships had multiple locations, and we were aggressive advertisers. Our monthly ad budget was well into six figures. These were the days prior to online advertising, so we were frequently seen across newspapers, TV and radio.

We were approached by a company whose specialty was deep-diving into our media and letting us know where our most effective campaigns were. It was a very expensive and lengthy project where, among other things, they interviewed our customers as well as those of our competitors about perceptions, where they heard about us, etc. Everyone involved in our advertising decisions was solidly convinced their ideas would come out on top.

The end result was quite shocking. Of all of the money we spent on conventional media, the number one way that customers found out about us or were aware of us was by seeing our license plate frames around the tags of vehicles we had sold. Millions were spent each year and a plastic, one-dollar frame was what was best getting the job done. It was evident that we were blindfolded, throwing very expensive darts at a board. It was clear that we needed help from experts.

In today's world, social media has created many new opportunities and more ways to reach prospects, but it has also created new challenges and needed skill sets. Advice from experienced pros can make your messages more effective and maximize your budget.

Advertising and marketing in today's world are terms that are usually intertwined with branding or building the image and reputation of your business. Social media provides a wonderful and valuable potential tool to accomplish this goal, but having the skills to navigate Facebook, X (Twitter), Instagram, TikTok, Pinterest and others are needed to make your venture successful.

It's a lot to grasp, so we reached out to one of the preeminent authorities in the social media and advertising fields, Dan Williamson, Founder and CEO of Louisville, KY's ProMedia Group. His firm was one of the first in the advertising field to recognize the role social media would play in branding and promotion. He graciously provided the following.

SOCIAL MEDIA TIPS for SMALL BUSINESS OWNERS

In an era dominated by digital communication and online networking, business owners of all generations need to embrace the power of social media. For Baby Boomer entrepreneurs, diving into the world of hashtags and tweets may seem daunting at first, but with the right guidance, they can leverage these platforms to enhance their business presence.

Here are some tips to help you shine on social media:

1. **Start slow and learn gradually:** For those who didn't grow up with smartphones and constant connectivity, the world of social media can be overwhelming. The key is to start slow and gradually build your understanding.

2. **Choose the right platform for your brand:** Begin with one or two platforms that align with your business goals. Facebook and LinkedIn are excellent starting points for professional networking and building a community around your brand, although you might want to consider Instagram if your product is more visual or X if you have time-specific announcements.

3. **Know your audience and use a voice that will resonate with them:** Take the time to identify and understand your target audience. Knowing the preferences and habits of your potential customers will help you tailor your social media content to better engage with them. We all want to believe that our product or service is universally loved. However, it's most likely that your customer demographic tells a different story. Find your people, talk to them, and grow what you know.

4. **Tell your story authentically and use original content:** You are the best one at telling your story and sharing your experience, so be candid about your

5. **Utilize visual content**: Visual content tends to be more engaging on social media platforms. Invest time in creating eye-catching visuals, whether it's images, infographics, or short videos. Platforms like Instagram and Pinterest are particularly visual-centric and can help showcase the visual aspects of your business. You only have a few seconds to grab someone's attention, so make sure you're making an impact from the jump.

6. **Leverage video**: Video is the best and easiest way to tell your story. Whether you're going live, making a Reel, or sharing a long-form video, make sure that the video is clear and conveys the correct message.

7. **Know your tools**: The right resources will help you refine your message. Explore what tools are at your fingertips (design software, scheduling software, AI) and recognize when it's time to lean on a professional, such as a marketing agency or videographer.

8. **Remain consistent:** Consistency is your best tool, but it is often overlooked. Don't let engagement or impression data lead you to believe that your message isn't valuable. Consistent messaging builds trust and dependability. How many times have you visited a social media page for a brand and questioned if they were still in business because they hadn't posted in a while?

9. **Don't be a nuisance:** Frequency is appreciated but bombarding your audience with a message is a sinking strategy. Refine the times that you post to when your audience is most active. Make sure your message is clear and that you are giving your audience enough time to process the information you are dispersing. Recognize when you are posting too much before they hit the snooze button, or worse...the unfollow.

10. **Paint a uniform picture with your brand:** All of your marketing initiatives should complement each other and follow the same brand guide. Your brand is a visual representation of your business, so people should be able to immediately recognize your marketing materials as yours. This includes your message. If you are running a special on social media, is your website updated to

mention this? Are your ads tailored to your special? Are your in-store print materials representative of your online presence?

11. **Make sure all of your platforms are connected:** Every platform gives you the ability to connect your other accounts so that people can easily find you. Make sure that your bio or about section highlights all the places people can find you on the internet.

12. **Embrace hashtags strategically**: Hashtags can significantly increase the visibility of your posts. Research and use relevant hashtags that align with your industry and target audience. Don't overdo it—aim for a balance between popular and niche hashtags to maximize your reach without appearing spammy.

13. **Engage with your audience**: Social media is a two-way street. Respond to comments, messages, and mentions promptly. Engaging with your audience not only builds a sense of community but also boosts the visibility of your content. Showcasing your commitment to customer interaction can set you apart in a positive way. *Note: Be sure who is responding to messages and that they are responding in a tone and manner that represents your brand. An off-handed comment from an upset employee can really cause damage.*

14. **Leverage LinkedIn for professional networking:** LinkedIn is a powerful tool for professional networking. Connect with other businesses, industry leaders, and potential clients. Participate in relevant groups and discussions to establish your expertise and expand your professional network.

15. **Invest in social media advertising:** Consider allocating a budget for social media advertising. Platforms like Facebook and Instagram offer targeted advertising options that can help you

reach a specific demographic. Paid promotions can increase your brand's visibility and drive traffic to your business.

While the digital landscape may seem foreign to some Baby Boomer business owners, the benefits of a strong social media presence cannot be overstated. By following these tips and gradually integrating social media into your business strategy, you can connect with a wider audience, showcase your experience, and ensure your business thrives in the digital age.

Chapter 30

Human Resources

HR is an area where small business owners tend to lack expertise. It isn't a skill set that we use each day, like inventory management or marketing. It can, however, be one of the most vital tools in our box. A lack of HR knowledge can also create additional and expensive problems that we don't need to add to our already full plates.

It is important for all business owners and managers to be current on employment law at the federal, state, and local levels.

Interviewing applicants, for example, would seem to be a great deal like two new friends getting to know each other. Questions about whether someone has children, is married, where they go to church, and the like would be common with a new friend; however, with a job applicant, those types of questions are illegal and can put you, the business owner, in a large pot of hot water. Knowing what you can and can't ask in an interview is vital information.

Dealing with your current staff comes with standards that are not only required by law, but just good practices. I recall years ago a General Manager in our organization that would use profanity in meetings. The company's founder had taken steps to train all of our managers in HR good practices, having a firm come in twice a year to work with managers on what they could and couldn't do.

This particular GM insisted that we were asking him to be someone other than who he truly was by watching his language. The founder, a very wise man, told him to pick words he could afford because if employees sued us for a hostile work environment because of his behavior, they would also sue him personally, and we wouldn't cover defending him. He departed soon after. That was a bullet dodged.

To give you a better insight into the many facets of HR, we reached out to a top expert, Amy Letke. Amy is the Founder & CEO of Integrity HR and is the National Human Resource Practice Leader for Marsh McLennan Agency in Louisville, Kentucky. She kindly provided the following.

Nurturing Your Dream Team: From Hiring to Engagement

Hey there, fellow small business owners! In this chapter, we'll dive into the nitty-gritty of hiring, counseling, and creating a positive work environment. Having owned several small businesses, I know how important it is to build a strong team that shares your vision and values. So, let's roll up our sleeves and explore the ins and outs of managing your employees with integrity and care.

Hiring the Right Fit

When it comes to hiring staff, finding the right fit for your small business is like finding the perfect puzzle piece. Here are some do's and don'ts to guide you along the way:

- Do: Clearly define the job requirements and qualifications and have job descriptions for every role in the organization. This will help you attract candidates who possess the necessary skills and experience. For example, when we were hiring a social media manager for one of our clients, we made sure to specify that we needed someone with experience in content creation, a knack for storytelling, and a passion for fashion. We wrote several job ads designed to attract candidates who were interested in these topics, using different keywords and modified the ads weekly to help us attract the right candidate that would fit our requirements. This helped us find someone who truly understood our brand and could connect with our target audience.

- Don't: Rely solely on resumes and interviews. Sometimes, you need to see a candidate in action to know if they're the right fit. Consider implementing skills assessments or trial periods to gauge their abilities firsthand. For example, When we were hiring a barista for our coffee shop client, we invited the top candidates to spend a few hours working alongside our team. This allowed us (the recruiters) and the client to see how the prospective employee interacted with customers, handled pressure, and crafted delicious beverages. And it gave the candidate a 'real life' example of what the job would entail. At the end of the day and after a few "job previews," we were able to have several candidates who were a great fit, and also wanted to be part of the team.

- Do: Conduct thorough background checks and reference checks. It's important to verify a candidate's credentials and ensure they have a track record of ethical behavior. When we were hiring a bookkeeper for our accounting firm client, we reached out to previous employers to get a sense of their reliability, attention to detail, and trustworthiness. This gave us peace of mind, knowing that we were bringing someone on board who would handle our clients' finances with care. Sometimes it can be tricky seeking references – one way to avoid the struggle of reaching an employer is to ask the candidate to help. Specifically, ask the candidate to supply you or the hiring manager with 2 or 3 professional references; have them reach out to those references ahead of time, indicating a prospective employer is going to contact them to discuss their prior work history and to request that the reference accept the phone call. Placing the responsibility of "setting up the reference" provides the opportunity to see how accountable the candidate is to provide the references, follow through with prior employers, and create a convenient way to introduce a conversation about their past work experiences.

Ethical Employee Management

Treating your employees ethically is the foundation of a healthy work environment, and it sets the foundation for the organization's culture, principles, and expectations. As I reflect on relationships in the workplace, a few specific actions can go a long way to creating an environment of positive relationships at work.

1. **Lead by example:** Your actions speak louder than words. Show integrity, fairness, and respect in everything you do, and your team will follow suit. One of our clients, the owner of a construction company, always made it a point to treat her crew with respect and fairness. She was not afraid to get her hands dirty alongside her team and always made sure they had the necessary safety equipment to do their jobs.

2. **Establish clear policies:** Develop a code of conduct that outlines expected behavior and ethical standards for all employees. One of our clients, a digital marketing agency, created a policy that emphasized honesty and transparency in our client interactions, providing specific examples to help employees understand where there could be dangerous interactions – their message was to be clear that we don't engage in any deceptive practices or make false promises, and employees were expected to do the same.

3. **Encourage open communication:** Create a safe space for employees to voice concerns or report unethical behavior without fear of retaliation. Some ways to accomplish this is to set aside time for open discussions during small group meetings, allowing employees time to share their thoughts, ideas, and any concerns they may have. Some clients go a step further and engage with a third party, where employees can report concerns without fear of retaliation and where an outside resource handles the complaint to bring it to closure.

Effective Corrective Action and Documentation

Disciplining employees is never easy, but it's necessary for maintaining a harmonious work environment, retaining team members who are high performers and dealing with poor performers as well. Here are a few tips for how you can handle disciplinary situations effectively.

Clearly communicate expectations

From day one, make sure employees are aware of your company's policies, job responsibilities and performance standards, which sets the foundation for accountability. At the onset of hiring, it is critical to provide each new team member with a detailed employee handbook that clearly outlines expectations regarding attendance, teamwork, and meeting designated deadlines. The employee handbook should cover federal, state and local employment laws and explain laws/policies clearly and effectively. A well-written employee handbook can serve as a guide to managers for handling a variety of situations and explain the expectations for compliance and adhering to these policies. Be certain to update the employee handbook every two years, and ensure each employee acknowledges receipt and understanding of the handbook in writing.

Addressing issues promptly

When performance or behavior concerns arise, it's critical to "not let them linger" and address them promptly and privately, providing constructive feedback and offering support to help employees improve. If an employee consistently misses project deadlines, schedule a one-on-one meeting to discuss the issue - approach the conversation with empathy, seeking to understand any challenges they may be facing. Then, develop a plan to improve their time management skills and meet project goals.

Document everything

Keeping detailed records of disciplinary situations is crucial! This documentation serves as evidence of your efforts to address the issue and protects your business in case of legal disputes. One of our clients had an employee who repeatedly violated the social media policy by posting inappropriate content. We helped the client document each incident, including screenshots of the posts and our subsequent conversations with the employee. This helped us demonstrate our commitment to addressing the issue and taking appropriate action. Always keep written records filed confidentially, providing copies of formal documentation to the employee as well.

Counseling for Improved Performance

Counseling employees for improved performance is an opportunity to support their growth and development, and your approach to handling the counseling is the key to setting the stage for positive discussions.

1. Create a safe and supportive environment

Let your employees know that counseling sessions are meant to help them succeed, not to criticize or punish them and encourage open communication and active listening. An example one of our clients did to demonstrate this occurred when an employee was struggling to meet sales targets at their retail store, they scheduled a private meeting to discuss their challenges. Their approach to the conversation was with empathy, seeking to understand any obstacles the employee may be facing. Following the conversation, they were able to jointly develop a plan to improve sales techniques and boost the employee's confidence.

2. Set clear goals and expectations

Work with employees to collaboratively establish performance goals and provide guidance on how to achieve them, reviewing progress and offering constructive feedback along the way. One way to accomplish this is through monthly check-ins with each team member to discuss their individual goals and provide feedback on their projects. This helps "the boss" as well as the employee stay focused and motivated to deliver their best work.

3. Provide resources and training

Periodically, it can be valuable to review team member's skills gaps for the purpose of enhancing performance, enriching jobs, and strengthening the engagement of employees. When we invest in employee development, it can greatly benefit both the individual and the business as well. When one of our client's customer service team was struggling with handling difficult customer interactions, we organized a training session on effective communication and conflict resolution techniques. This equipped them with the skills and confidence to handle challenging situations with grace and helped the team by offering real situations to "practice" in a safe environment.

Crafting Effective Social Media Policies

In the age of "every day is a social media day," having a well-defined policy is crucial to help employees stay on track at work and protect your business as well. Here are some key elements to include in a policy:

1. **Clarify acceptable behavior** Clearly outline what is considered appropriate and inappropriate when it comes to social media usage. Encourage employees to use social media responsibly and respect confidentiality. As an example, one of our client's social media policies states that employees should" refrain from posting negative comments about our competitors or sharing confidential company information, and emphasizes the importance of maintaining a positive online presence that aligns with our brand values."

2. **Protect your brand:** Remind employees that their actions on social media can reflect on your company's reputation and encourage them to represent your business positively online. We had an incident where an employee posted a negative review about a client's product on their personal social media account – we used this as an opportunity to educate our team about the importance of maintaining professionalism and avoiding public criticism.

3. **Address privacy concerns:** Inform employees about the importance of respecting customer privacy and confidentiality. Provide guidelines on handling sensitive information and avoiding the disclosure of proprietary or confidential data.

Building a Positive Company Culture and Promoting Employee Engagement

Creating a positive company culture and fostering employee engagement are essential for attracting and retaining top talent. Here are some strategies to consider to develop a positive culture within your organization:

1. Encourage teamwork and collaboration:

Foster a sense of camaraderie by promoting teamwork and collaboration among employees. Some of the most memorable team engagement experiences included visiting an "escape room," a gun range, and even a downtown scavenger hunt – our team still talks about our annual "team day" experiences that created a personal connection with each employee. As I reflect on this, it really helped to foster and develop a supportive work environment where everyone feels valued and connected.

2. Recognize and reward achievements:

Find ways to celebrate employee accomplishments to boost morale and motivation- it doesn't take much to say "thank you" and show genuine appreciation. Over the years, what I've found is "what gets scheduled, gets done." In the area of employee recognition, if you can schedule periodic times to provide recognition for great performance, for anniversaries, for birthdays and "wins," it can bring team members together and feel more connected to the business leader(s) and purpose. One of our clients even recognizes outstanding performance at the end of each month with a "Star of the Month" award. This recognition not only boosts the recipient's confidence but also inspires others to strive for excellence.

3. Provide growth opportunities:

Offer professional development opportunities and career advancement paths to show employees that you value their growth. This doesn't need to be expensive or require a tremendous time investment, but it can help retain employees when their job and experience is enriched. A simple way to provide for growth is to include employees when attending industry conferences, providing opportunities for "free" online courses, and even creating internal mentorship programs. This investment in employee development not only enhances skills valuable to the business but also fosters loyalty and commitment to your company.

Navigating National Employment Laws

Understanding national employment laws is crucial for small business owners to avoid legal risks.

Here are some key laws to be aware of:

1. **Fair Labor Standards Act (FLSA):** This law governs minimum wage, overtime pay, and child labor standards. To comply, understand the requirements and properly classify employees. Risk: Misclassifying employees as exempt from overtime pay can lead to costly lawsuits. The simplest way to comply is to review the FLSA guidelines and consult legal professionals or HR experts if needed.

2. **Family and Medical Leave Act (FMLA):** Familiarize yourself with the FMLA to provide eligible employees with job-protected leave for qualified medical and family reasons. Risk: Failing to provide eligible employees with FMLA leave or retaliating against them for taking leave can result in legal consequences.

The simplest way to comply is to understand the FMLA requirements and establish policies that align with the law.

3. **Equal Employment Opportunity (EEO) Laws:** These laws prohibit discrimination based on factors such as race, gender, religion, and disability. To comply, implement fair hiring practices and maintain a workplace free from discrimination. Risk: Discrimination claims can damage your business's reputation and result in legal action. The simplest way to comply is to ensure your hiring practices are fair, provide equal opportunities for all employees, and establish a no-tolerance policy for discrimination.

Managing your employees effectively requires a combination of ethical practices, clear communication, and a supportive work environment. Consider the value of implementing a few of the strategies and principles discussed in this chapter, and you'll be well on your way to nurturing a dream team that propels your small business to success. Remember, building a positive company culture and complying with employment laws go hand in hand. Stay informed about national employment laws, seek professional advice when needed, and prioritize the well-being and growth of your employees.

Chapter 31

Best Use of Video to Promote Your Brand

Video is one of the most powerful tools to help you build your brand and customer base, yet it is still underutilized. For example, according to a study published by Wyzowl in 2024, 69% of customers believe that a video product demo best assists them when making a purchase. Yet, only 47% of marketers invest in product demos.

Most viewers believe that user-generated content, or content produced by the company themselves as opposed to an agency, is the most genuine form of advertising. Shoppable ads, or those that have clickable buttons that take the viewer directly to a page where they can purchase the item or service, increase conversion rates by upto 70%.

70% of YouTube viewers have made a purchase after seeing a brand on YouTube. With the platform having 70 BILLION daily video views, that is certainly a lot of commerce. Facebook and Instagram also reach into the billions.

For some expert advice, we reach out to Tracy Misner. In addition to years of teaching video to students, he operates a very successful video business in Winston-Salem, NC. He shared some tips to make your videos more effective.

10 Practical Tips for Using Video

1. Think about your MESSAGE first and shorten your message as much as possible with your focus solely on your audience. When

using video, it is very important that you understand that you are making your video for your audience–not for you! Who is the audience–are they young, old, male, or female–what is your demographic and cater that message to that audience? If you think your message is for everyone–think again–it's not! For example, are you catering your message to your local audience or is it for people in Europe, in Asia? Say only what you need to say. Social media videos should never exceed 30 seconds unless it's a slickly produced video!

2. If you say it, show it–if you show it, say it! If you are talking about a service you provide, show that service in action. If you're showing your service in action, describe to the audience what they are seeing. We don't need to see you walking into your office and seeing people on the phone—we want to see you cut hair, do makeup, clean gutters, paint a house, cut the grass, clean a car.

3. Think about AUDIO! Your video is 50% audio–if we cannot hear you clearly, your audience will leave quicker than you think! You MUST use a good microphone and be in a quiet place to say what you need to say. I recommend Rode wireless or Rode on-camera microphones

4. Think about VIDEO! Your video must be stable, steady, clean and clear! Use a tripod. If you are using your phone to film–use a tripod. Amazon sells tons of iPhone holders for tripods–they are about $5.00!

5. Think about LIGHTING! Do not film yourself against windows. Do not film in a dark room. Video needs a lot of light. Film outside during the day in a shady area–the sunlight will be plenty for you if you choose the right location–avoid very sunny spots.

6. Think about your BACKGROUND! Watch for things like trash cans, people behind you, graffiti (think bad words), or worse–animals–we've all seen these pictures on the internet–don't be one of those.

7. Only film ONE person at a time–never two people. Only one of you can talk at a time anyway–the other person may look awkward standing there waiting for you to finish what you have to say.

8. You can start out very easily on your phone, but remember audio and video are super important–don't pan the camera left and right to show a room—that's called firehosing–do not firehose!

9. Remember to smile when you talk–even if this takes you ten tries to get it right–a smile goes a very long way.

10. Clothes, grooming- Do not wear any visible brands and do not wear anything political–clothes need to be simple with dark colors (avoid red). Make sure your hair is combed or brushed, have done light makeup if needed–you want people to hear your message, not laugh at what you are wearing!

11. Bonus: Hire a professional videographer if you are very concerned with your brand/message/story–you'll know if it's the right time. Questions answered should be FREE!

Chapter 32

Pushing Through Success While Balancing Life's Obligations

From Cheryl Dacey

As an entrepreneur, you are no stranger to the grind. You've put in countless hours building your business, often at the expense of other important parts of your life. Between long workdays, networking events, and trying to keep up with the ever-changing digital landscape, it can feel like there's hardly any time left for your spouse, kids, aging parents, or your own well-being.

I get it - I've been there. For over 22 years, I was a high-powered corporate sales executive, working 60+ hour weeks and traveling constantly. During that time, I also started and operated several traditional businesses in the hospitality industry and a very successful network marketing business. Now, I help people build thriving online businesses through digital marketing. Through it all, I've had to learn how to balance the demands of entrepreneurship with the needs of my family and personal life. It's certainly not easy, but it is possible.

The key is to approach your life with intention and make a conscious effort to be present, regardless of what you're doing. When you're working on your business, be 100% focused on it. And when you're with your loved ones, be fully engaged with them, not constantly checking your phone or thinking about your to-do list. It takes discipline and practice, but it's so worth it.

Start by time-blocking your calendar. Dedicate specific hours of the day to business activities and guard that time fiercely. Then, make sure to also block off time for your personal life - date nights, family dinners, kids' activities, exercise, etc. Treat these personal commitments with the same level of importance as you would a client meeting or important deadline.

You may need to get creative to make it all fit. Consider waking up an hour earlier to get a head start on your day, or batch processing certain tasks to be more efficient. I'm a big believer in the Pomodoro Technique - working in focused 25-minute sprints with short breaks in between. It helps me stay on track and avoid burnout.

And don't be afraid to ask for help when you need it. Enlist your spouse or older kids to pitch in with household chores or errands. Hire a virtual assistant to handle administrative tasks. Take advantage of AI and digital marketing tools. Outsource anything that's not your zone of genius. The more you can delegate, the more time and energy you'll have to dedicate to your most important priorities.

Of course, being an entrepreneur means that your schedule will never be 100% predictable. There will always be fires to put out and unexpected challenges to overcome. That's why it's crucial to nurture your resilience and keep your "why" front and center. Remind yourself daily of the deeper purpose behind your business - is it to create generational wealth? To make a positive impact on your community? To model entrepreneurship for your children?

Whenever you feel pulled in a million directions, pause and reconnect with that driving force. Let it infuse your actions and give you the strength to push through. And don't forget to weave in moments of joy and celebration, too. Take a walk/dance break in the middle of the workday. Plan a weekend getaway with your spouse. Savor a quiet cup of coffee before the kids wake up. These little pockets of pleasure will help you stay grounded and inspired.

Most importantly, be kind to yourself. There will be days when you feel like you're failing at everything. That's okay - we all have those moments. The key is to not let them snowball. Acknowledge your feelings, then redirect your focus to what's going well. Celebrate small wins, and remember that your worth is not defined by how productive you are.

As an entrepreneur, you're on a wild ride. There will be exhilarating highs and exhausting lows. But through it all, stay committed to your vision and don't lose sight of what really matters. Your family, your health, your spiritual well-being - those are the foundations upon which a truly successful life is built.

So keep going, my friend. The world needs your gifts. And remember, you're not alone. I'm in your corner, cheering you on every step of the way.

Here are 5 more tips to help you push through success while navigating life's many responsibilities:

1. **Prioritize self-care:** It's easy to let your own needs fall to the wayside when you're juggling so much. But taking care of yourself has to be a non-negotiable. Schedule regular exercise, healthy meals, and time for hobbies and relaxation. This will give you the energy and resilience to show up as your best self in all areas of life.

2. **Communicate openly:** Be transparent with your loved ones about the demands of running a business. Involve them in the process and get their buy-in. This will help manage expectations

and reduce conflict down the line. Plus, your family may surprise you with their willingness to pitch in and support your entrepreneurial journey.

3. **Learn to delegate and let go:** As a high-achieving entrepreneur, it can be tempting to try to do everything yourself. But that's a surefire path to burnout. Identify the tasks you can hand off to others, whether it's hiring support staff or outsourcing certain business functions. Then, resist the urge to micromanage - trust the people you've brought onto your team.

4. **Embrace the power of no:** It's okay to turn down opportunities or requests that don't align with your priorities. In fact, it's essential. Get comfortable setting boundaries and saying no to things that will pull you away from your most important goals and responsibilities. Your time and energy are precious - protect them fiercely.

5. **Find an accountability partner:** Having someone in your corner who can champion you, offer a fresh perspective, and keep you on track can make all the difference. This could be a business coach, a mastermind group, or even a trusted friend or family member. Lean on them when you need an extra boost of motivation or encouragement.

Cheryl Dacey is a trailblazing executive and entrepreneurial powerhouse with a career spanning over three decades. Her journey through the corporate landscape reads like a masterclass in versatility and innovation, leaving an indelible mark on the telecom, hospitality, wellness, and healthcare sectors.

With an impressive track record of awards and accolades, Cheryl's expertise isn't confined to the boardroom. Her entrepreneurial spirit has led her to successfully grow two distinct hospitality brands while simultaneously achieving top 1% leadership status within a prominent direct sales organization.

As the visionary CEO and Founder of The Dacey Group, Cheryl channels her passion for helping others achieve time and financial freedom. Her mission? To revolutionize how businesses approach their finances and operations.

Epilogue

At the end of the day, achieving business success is often more art than science. While intuition and strong people skills can take you far, practical knowledge and experience are invaluable. If I could leave you with just a handful of insights, I'd consider it a triumph.

First and foremost, never underestimate the value of the people around you. Strive to create opportunities for their growth and development. When your team feels important and included in your mission, your business performance will reflect that commitment.

Remember, profitability is the cornerstone of all your aspirations. Keep a close eye on your expenses, profit margins, and sales figures. Understanding what it takes to keep your bottom line on the positive side of break-even is essential for sustainability.

It's crucial to recognize that doing the right thing and taking the easy path are seldom the same. Choose integrity, even when it feels like it costs you something in the short run. You'll ultimately find that the rewards of doing the right thing are far more valuable.

Give back to your community. Investing your time in service often yields benefits that far exceed the contributions you make to the causes you support.

Celebrate your victories, no matter how small, and embrace your failures as important learning opportunities. Remember, something that initially appears to be a setback can offer invaluable lessons that pave the way for future success.

Thank you for reading. I hope my thoughts and experiences have provided helpful guidance for you and your business.

A heartfelt thank you to the talented individuals who contributed to this work. Your insights and expertise have enriched this book significantly. Special thanks to my friend Henry Ball for his keen proofreading and for being an exceptional sounding board throughout this process, and to Susan Daniel, for continuing to take my calls when I know I have likely worn out my welcome!

Finally, to my wife, Marian: your positivity, support, and unwavering belief in me have made this journey possible. You truly are the greatest gift of my life.

Author's Bio

Jim Harris:

From Car Dealerships to Bestselling Author

Jim Harris isn't just another business writer—he's a small business alchemist who turns struggling ventures into gold mines. With over four decades of experience, Jim's career reads like a playbook for success in the cutthroat world of entrepreneurship.

The Early Years: Selling Dreams on Four Wheels

Imagine being the new kid on the block, surrounded by seasoned pros. That was Jim in his first auto sales job at nineteen. But instead of being intimidated, he blazed past the competition, selling a staggering thirty+ cars a month when the national average was eight and being the dealership's top performer. This wasn't beginner's luck—raw talent colliding with relentless drive.

The Midas Touch: Turning Dealerships Around

Jim's management career is a highlight reel of business transformations:

- **Ford**: Catapulted a dealership from last place of six in the metro area to first, boosting volume by 500% and profits by over 1000%.
- **Chevrolet**: Repeated the magic, taking another underdog from last of nine to the top spot with a tenfold profit increase.
- **Chrysler Dodge**: Hat-trick achieved! Yet another worst-to-first turnaround with record-breaking profits.

The crown jewel? In 2006, Jim bought a Chrysler Dodge Jeep dealership in Atlanta that was hemorrhaging money. The half-dozen previous owners couldn't get close to breaking even, let alone make a profit. Jim's solution? He built a dream team from scratch and netted a $130,000 profit in the first month, skyrocketing the dealership into the top five of thirty dealers in metro sales.

Diversifying the Portfolio: From Iron to Iron-Pumping

Not content with conquering the auto world, Jim and his wife launched a personal training business from their garage in 2013. Within two years, with just the two of them, they were pulling in mid-six figures and expanding to multiple locations. Their clients' success stories didn't just make newspapers and magazines—they made it into the United States Congressional Record!

The Digital Frontier: Blogs, Podcasts, and Beyond

Retirement? Not for Jim. He's now:

- A prolific writer with articles featured in publications across the Southeastern U.S.
- Creator of "The Southern Voice," a blog with millions of readers.
- Host of "Rock Stars Talk," a podcast that shot to #3 in the U.S. in its first season.

Giving Back

Following Muhammad Ali's wisdom about service to others, Jim's philanthropy is as impressive as his business acumen:

- Board member for non-profits like the Leukemia and Lymphoma Society.
- Fundraising powerhouse for various charities.
- Active participant in Christmas Child and Toys for Tots.
- Champion for law enforcement, homeless populations, foster children, and veterans.

A Collaborative Masterpiece: "The Small Biz Guide"

What sets "The Small Biz Guide" apart isn't just Jim's wealth of experience—it's his recognition that true wisdom comes from many sources. Jim has curated a dream team of experts and thought leaders across various business disciplines to create a comprehensive resource unlike any other.

In this groundbreaking book, you'll find:

- Marketing and social media pros sharing cutting-edge strategies for the digital age.
- Financial wizards offering insights on funding, cash flow management, and sustainable growth.
- HR experts providing guidance on building and nurturing high-performing teams.
- Tech gurus demystifying the latest tools and technologies for small businesses.
- Tax experts with advice to safely minimize your liability.
- Leasing experts to help you get the right terms in the best location.
- Work-life balance coaches sharing strategies for "having it all" – success in business and a fulfilling personal life.

"The Small Biz Guide" is a one-stop shop for entrepreneurs at any stage of their journey.

Why "The Small Biz Guide" is Your Next Must-Read

Jim Harris doesn't just talk the talk—he's walked the walk-through countless business landscapes. Now, he's bringing you not just his own insights but the collective wisdom of a carefully selected group of industry experts. "The Small Biz Guide" distills decades of hard-earned wisdom into actionable advice that could differentiate between your business merely surviving or thriving.